TERROR-REST

About Highland Books

Find out more about us and our other publications on our website: www.highlandbks.com.
If you see a mistake you can e-mail us at errata@highlandbks.com.
There is also a book-related site: www.terror-rest.net

TERROR-REST

Psalm 91:
God's prayer
of protection
for you and
your family

Ed Morris

Godalming, Surrey

First published in Great Britain in 2006
by Highland Books,
Two High Pines, Knoll Road
GODALMING, Surrey GU7 2EP

ISBN: 1 897913 70 2

Cover design by Steve Carroll

Printed in Finland for HIGHLAND BOOKS
by Bookwell Oy.

Contents

DEDICATION

Dedicated to the memory
of all who died in
the Lockerbie disaster

THANKS

To the Rev John Webster

My Father and Mother who introduced me
to Psalm 91 and the story angle

PREFACE

London, December 1988. I am saying goodbye to an Italian girl I have been getting to know for a few months. She has invited me for dinner in South Kensington and shown me her collection of timepieces.

"I am off to America." she says

"Send me a card!"

"Back in three weeks."

"Great ! See you then!"

"Ciao."

"Ciao."

January 1989 passed with no card. I began to conclude the dinner-date was too much for her and maybe the *ciao* was more permanent. One day in February, I remember quite clearly, I walked past where she worked in Piccadilly. Male pride got the better of me so I popped in just to say hello! I ran up the stairs into the office in anticipation, only to see another girl sitting there.

I said, "Is Gianfranca around?"

"—No! Haven't you heard?"

"No! What?"

"She's dead! She was on the plane … Lockerbie …"

Hatred! The word has an old-fashioned ring in our age of political correctness. But it refers to an emotional reality which the Bible and indeed all religions are well aware of.

Jesus warned his disciples to expect to be hated, because the world hated him first. Famously, he also commanded his followers to love their enemies, but this book is not about that healing response,

It is about those fearful emergencies when we face dangers: we are driving too fast on a wet motorway, and the tyres begin to lose contact; a dangerous gas is in the air; violence threatens personally or nationally. Persecution or temptation is warring on your spirit. Threats come from the natural world, from the devices man has invented, from other people or from the unseen world of the spirit.

Some use intimidation or violence methodically: the only peace they want is a piece of you. They want to hurt you and manipulate you through the fears they stir up. But sometimes their masks slip and we see them as they truly are: abusers, bullies anarchists or tyrants. They may even masquerade as angels of light but inside they are ravenous lions.

God knew that we would face real troubles, threats, wars, diseases, plagues and that is why he inspired one of his confidants to tell about the experience under the shadow of his protection. We know it as Psalm 91; the psalm contains the antidote to which we must entrust ourselves. For the poet faced all comers, viruses, diseases, plagues and overcame them with God.

The book is proposing a meditation and reflection on Psalm 91 that hopefully will inspire you to make it one of your daily prayers. Psalm 91 is not a mantra or a talisman against trouble. But taking it to heart as a cry for God's protection from within trouble may make all the difference between paralysis and faith. To encourage you I have thought up a 91-second/91-day challenge.

This first part of the book is 'my' story of Psalm 91. The second part is the analysis and positioning of the Psalm and applications. The third part of the book is a verse-by-verse meditation over 30 days plus my 91-second challenge. An appendix gives my ha'penny worth on terror.

How I was led to study Psalm 91

In my childhood my father tried to teach my brother and me self-defence via boxing, wrestling and judo but he seemed to realise the limitations of such methods given the nuclear war threat, Asian flu epidemic and *The Exorcist*. He then told us a story about a wartime Christian officer who gave a copy of Psalm 91 to each of his men; they all agreed to pray the psalm every day for protection throughout the hostilities. At the end of the campaign not one man was lost. Many years later came......

War! The newspaper I was reading considered the invasion of Iraq in 2003 as a few weeks away. All the airports were under maximum security – a ring of steel, the article seemed to say. But reading the back of a gentleman's *Times* was not easy on the Number 23 bus as it trundled along the streets. Suddenly, bang! A middle eastern looking gentleman looked up, everyone in the bus froze. It was a false alarm, just his briefcase which had overbalanced!

Overreaction? Yet moving along Oxford Street, there were unmistakable evidences of a city under pressure from violence, crime and terrorism. Surveillance cameras at every corner, security guards outside shops, red-hatted Community Officers on the beat and the police cars patrolling. Only the night before I had witnessed a phone theft, hand bag mugging and a chair being thrown across a bar as two men argued and abused each other. All to the intermittent background of flashing lights and music of police sirens, fire alarms and car horns interlaced with newspapers screaming out headlines; 'Bullied kid hangs himself', 'Woman, 87, mugged' and 'Bomb kills twelve'. They say that crime statistics in London are now worse than New York.

Later that day at Holy Communion: the church building was a rare oasis of tranquillity in a city of noise. The old priest shook my hand and I volunteered, "There's tension in London"

"Well London, we have seen it all before, the Blitz and the IRA bombs," he replied adding,

"In fact not far from here a colleague of mine was conducting Holy Communion when an IRA bomb blew up a restaurant. Since the chapel was near by the police asked him if he could perform last rites to the dying as the emergency forces attended the injured. He was in his white communion habit and went straight to the devastation. While he was attending a dying man and his wife, he noticed a few couples at their tables eating their meals as if nothing had happened. He asked a police man what about those people. The policeman said they were in a state of shock and are carrying on as if nothing had happened."

I said, "That is strange"

"Yes but even stranger," he carried on, "was that the blood of the innocent man who died had stained the white cassock of my priest friend and to this day no bleach, stain remover has ever been able to remove it."

"Stranger and stranger, it is like the blood of the innocent is still crying out for justice." I said.

"But there is one last detail. Unfortunately for the restaurant the IRA had targeted the wrong place so it was a needless bombing."

"Madness!" I said.

"Such is the nature of violence and vengeance."

"What is the answer, what is God's answer?" I asked.

"Within the Bible there is a prayer, a special prayer about a secret place where you can find real security. Within that place is an antidote that tells of a God who can be trusted at all times and in all circumstances and places no matter how hard the times. This God promises that his love will never separate from you. 'No in all these things we are more than conquerors through him who loved us. For I am convinced that neither death nor life, neither angels nor demons, neither the present nor the future, nor any powers, neither height or depth, nor anything else in all creation, will be able to separate us from the love of God that is in Christ Jesus our Lord.' This God can be trusted at all time – in even the worst imaginable crisis."

"Sure that was then, but now?" I suggested.

"No! Throughout history people have found safety in this prayer. In fact this is the writer's personal testimony of his own experience as a traveller who has negotiated some dangerous passages in his journey through life. Come for breakfast tomorrow and I will explain more."

Next morning was typical English February; people were bustling to get coffees, bacon and eggs and toast before going to work. A newspaper lay strewn across the table in the coffee bar where the old priest sat. The headline said '12 people killed in bombing'. In my mind there seemed an escalation in these events.

"We live in violent times and since September 11 the world seems to have gone crazy," said a man glaring at the headline while eating his breakfast at the table next to the old clergyman.

"The threat of violence, terror and war is real. What we face is unseen in delivery, uncertain in form and unknown in the target," said the lady sitting on our table.

"Yes, Madam! Just like this English breakfast I'm eating" said the man.

"Watch it," said the lady who was cooking the breakfast behind the counter.

Sitting down I said to the priest, "The incidence of violence in work, schools and neighbourhoods seems to be increasing."

The woman in the corner added; "Not only that but the type of tactics used can range from physical, psychological and emotional; while terrorist weapons can be conventional, chemical, biological and even nuclear."

The old clergyman said; "At least we do have some choices: we can run away or cover it up or face it. Sadly, this type of violence is not self-cancelling – you just don't know if it will erupt quickly or fester for a while."

"So how do we cope with such uncertainty or take the terror out of terrorism?"

"Yes, Madam and how do I survive this Great British Breakfast?" said the man as he got up to leave.

"I don't know why we let him in." said the lady chef to the waitress as the man went out the door.

"Within the Bible is an invitation: to the safest place in the world; from the wisest person in all the universe; for anyone who genuinely wishes to get there. All are welcome! It is the gift of a God who can be trusted at all times and in all circumstances, conditions and relationships. More importantly, it is a promise that this God's love will never separate from you. Walk through Psalm 91 with me!"

Many readers will be familiar with one or other translation of this psalm. I have enjoyed creating my very own version of the psalm versifying in oriental haiku style:

Live and stay up close,
where Almighty God Most High
shades and hides your base.

I say to the LORD,
"You're my refuge and fortress.
My God I trust you."

He will snap me out
of deadly curses and traps
set maliciously.

His feathers! His nest!
Underwing cover! Trust him,
His truth missile-proof.

You can stop fearing
covert night-time onslaughts or
daylight sniper fire.

No excuse to dread
dusk's demonic germ attack
or high noon mayhem.

Thousands fall near you
mass destruction on your right
—yet you're left unscathed.

Tough punishment falls
on sin-flawed wicked people:
You'll see justice done.

The LORD's your refuge
The Almighty God's your home.
Evil can't touch you.

God commands – angels,
guarding every turn – angels,
you slip-slide; they catch.

You'll stamp on poison
snakes, stop ravening lions:
yes, and dragons sprawl.

"Because he loves me,
I'll deliver him. My name
he knows I uphold.

He calls in distress.
I answer, stick close, rescue
—he shares the honours.

I'll grace him long life,
and then delight his eyes with
utmost salvation."

This version is presented as-is! If you have the
time to invest, and it is a worthwhile exercise in

itself, I invite you to create your own version of the psalm, haiku or otherwise. If you email me (info@terror-rest.net); I will consider posting it on the terror-rest.net website.

THE PROMISE

It was bright morning and we met at the chapel.

"So what is the promise?" the lady asked.

The priest answered, "Let me quote from a book from the First World War called *Fragment from the Trenches*, written by Thomas Tiplady, Chaplain to the Forces."

It was Thursday evening, in a little village behind the line, and the hour we had chosen for worship. There we found a quiet corner where the trees round us appeared like the pillars in the aisles of our churches at home... Then we bowed our heads, and I asked one or two of the men to lead in prayer- not knowing which would respond, but leaving them to the Spirit promptings. Quietly naturally, and with humility they lifted up their voices in prayer. Two prayed; three prayed I asked for more. It was so sweet to hear them that I could not bring myself to stop the music of their prayers. Five or six prayed; then came silence as thrilling as speech, and, after it, and to present it to his Father and ours. After the prayer the men chose a hymn. Then I read to them the 91st Psalm. 'He that dwelleth in the secret place of the Most High ...'

A few weeks later many of the men were to see 'the arrow that flieth by day', for suddenly shells fell like thunderbolts about their billets, killing and wounding many. They were also to feel 'the terror by night', for while out in front of their trenches, digging in the darkness, the foe discovered their presence and searched their ranks with shot and shell. But the Wings were over the lads who met for worship on that calm evening of which I write, and who, with faces lit by the setting sun, had listened to that psalm of confidence in God. They were saved from the arrow by day and the terror by night.

"That is the promise of Psalm 91. It is a complete promise against all the perils, terrors, attacks, pestilences, plagues, snares, slanders no matter when and where they occur which cause the fall of many but none need to be feared, the LORD's care is guaranteed. This comprehensive list is there to tell us there is nothing at all to fear although the threats may be acute, continuous or chronic – no exclusions, no hidden small print. Covering all times of the day, winter, spring, summer, autumn. If you confidently choose to entrust yourself like a child to dwell in the secret place of the Most High.

"No, this psalm hits right at of the heart of the violence and promises real safety as opposed to false safety. Psalm 91 takes into account that we are not in a shadow boxing contest but in a full contact brutal fight with adversaries whose very method requires injury, death and destruction as a way to promote their end. This cycle of mayhem and mischief takes place in a no-holds-barred environment. No Marquess of Queensberry rules or codes of conduct, so below-the-belt and rabbit punches are possible. No set time for starting, before the bell, after the bell. No set location, in the ring, out of the ring even in the changing room at speed, unseen and with maximum force coming from any angle or position. No human rights only inhumane fights. No Health and Safety rules either and no restriction on damage. No points win here, the outcome is by death, destruction and injury.

"Psalm 91 focuses on where to entrust your safety and what is real safety. For no human or scientific intelligence can anticipate and respond to the numerous mind-boggling dangers and complexities that this type of violence induces because it is multi dimensional and chaotic. Whereas the secret place where God is sought develops trust, poise and peace. It reminds me of a woman during the Blitz in World War 2. When she had not been to the shelter for several nights, people thought she was dead. They saw her walking around some days later and asked where she had been during the nights of constant explosions. She replied, 'I read the Bible and it said the LORD neither slumbers nor sleeps, and I didn't think there was any need for both of us to stay awake.'

"Psalm 91 doesn't negate adequate common sense protection neither does it condone presumptive behaviour rather it warns that our resources, information, strategies and tactics can be insufficient to take into account all the dangers we face – for we 'wrestle not against flesh and blood but against powers and principalities.'

"One problem we face is that we have been trained to be self-reliant and by nature self focused, so we can delude ourselves and place too much reliance on systems that protect ourselves on a narrow view of experience and on systems that respond at inappropriate levels to the reality. Humanly, we each have a breaking point beyond which we are paralysed by fear.

In recent times at the Houses of Parliament, the centre of power in the UK where security is at its most tight, the system was found lacking when protestors (fortunately peaceful) outflanked security and got on the other side of the protective shield. They sprinkled purple dye on the Prime Minister and Cabinet. A few weeks later a group of protestors gained access to the House of Commons, dashing right up to the Speaker of the House.

"By dwelling in the secret place, God's presence and refuge is guaranteed against anything that comes against you in your journey through life. The message of this prayer is that if faithfully prayed and believed then God the Almighty will protect you. You have his promise which you can count on.

"A few years ago the World Boxing Heavy-weight division was ruled by one of the most intimidating and ruthless of champions. Opponents regularly were despatched in early rounds. One day he was matched against a challenger who believed in Christ. By fixing his eyes on Jesus and believing that he could do all things through Jesus who gave him strength, this contender succeeded in knocking out the champion.

"Survey the sweep of history and you will see all tyrants and aggressors die in the end. What is sad is that so many people have lived the best part of their life in desperation because of them. The truth is that each generation produces such types. Psalm 91 illustrates that we the so-called powerless have the chance of getting the Almighty God on our side to protect us. Life is too short to live in perpetual fear."

The priest finished his talk. The gentleman, whom I recognised as the one who had complained about the breakfast earlier, asked who were the beneficiaries of this 'comprehensive promise'.

"Well, Sir," said the clergyman, "The glory of Psalm 91 is that it is for anyone, no matter what his temperament, character, psychology – or whatever you call it. This is not a hope for a certain kind of person; whosoever ...

---

whosoever comes! Yes, Sir, that's the invitation! Psalm 91 is for anyone who is or who feels themselves to be in danger. All are invited, all welcome and all accepted.

"There are three main classes of beneficiary:

1) Those who cannot forget past defeats and fear continued enslavement.

2) Those who have just been ambushed in the present and are in the thick of conflict.

3) Those who plan to set out on a dangerous expedition with known risks.

The aims are the same for all; protection, preservation and peace of mind in times of uncertainty. For those who want the grace of God when under pressure. But it is for the potential beneficiaries to claim on the policy at the critical moment. They should also avoid the 'contributory negligence' of failing to familiarise themselves with God's hiding place."

"Are there any exclusions?" enquired the Lady Chef looking at the man who ate the breakfast.

"Did you know that this is the only scripture quoted by God, Jesus and the Devil? The Devil tried to tempt Jesus to test God's faithfulness by jumping from a great height so that God's angels would catch him. Jesus saw through this and said it was wrong to test God. Those who are not covered are those who recklessly test God."

The priest leaned back and said, "I would like to propose a trip to deepen our experience of this promise."

One Secret Place

The house was located at 19 Bartlejorisstraat at the centre of Haarlem, Holland. The old priest was waiting outside with the others.

"Welcome, I'm glad you could make it."

"So you are going to show us the secret place," I said.

"Yes the hiding place."

He smiled knowingly.

"A long way to come, that's all I say!" said the man.

The lady stared disapprovingly at the man and then said, "It looks like a watch shop and museum to me."

"Since 1837 the ground floor has been a home to one family and a seller of watches. It has also been turned into a museum. Let's go in," said the old priest.

In the dining room was an oval table and an open Bible.

"Around this table sat the Ten Boom family, aunts, parents, children, foster children, generations of them. During World War 2 it was where Jews sat who were on Hitler's extermination list and on the run from the Gestapo."

"What you mean the Ten Boom family hid these people from the Nazis?" I said.

"Yes!"

"Look the Family Bible is open on Psalm 91," said the lady; *"Die in de schuilplaats des Allerhoogsten is gezeten ...* He who dwells in the secret place of the Most High ..."

"Let's go to Corrie Ten Boom's room."

Behind a false wall was an area where Jews were hidden: a small hiding place, but as long as they hid there they were safe.

The priest continued, "In Corrie Ten Boom's book *The Hiding Place* she tells of a story where one day there was a Gestapo raid and two members of the Dutch Underground plus four Jews were rushed into this small space. They entered through the sliding door located at the bottom of the linen closet. They remained in this space for 47 hours until rescued by the Underground. The hiding place saved their lives."

"What happened to Corrie Ten Boom?" asked the man.

"Corrie herself was put into an extermination camp but placed herself in God's hiding place. By God's miracle she was released. She learned that there is no pit so deep that it exceeds the depth of God's love and God will enable you to forgive your enemies. Afterwards she had a world wide mission helping people of all sorts.

Corrie died on her 91st birthday 15th April 1983; according to Jewish tradition it is only very blessed people who are allowed the privilege to die on their birthday. 800 Jews were delivered from Nazi hands by the Ten Boom family. In her house was a small hiding place. As long as they were there they were safe.

As I walked out I glanced once more at her father's Bible opened at Psalm 91.

Outside the priest said, "Jesus taught about the secret place, 'but when you pray, go into your most private room and closing the door, pray to your father who is in secret; and your father who sees in secret will reward you in the open'. In the Old Testament the secret place was found in the temple in the courtyard of which stood the altar of burnt offerings where the blood of bulls and lambs was shed. The outer court is where the blood was spilt and applied to the worshippers' sins. Then there were the lavers and mirrors and washbowls where they could wash and see themselves as clean. The next compartment was the Holy Place, then the Holy of Holies. It is here where the High Priest had the privilege to enter in. Under the New Covenant all believers in Christ have boldness to enter into the Holy of Holies by the blood of Jesus."

A different Secret Place

Here is a second take coming from a more meditative tradition:

> Be brave and walk through the country of your own wild heart. Be gentle and know that you know nothing. Be mindful and remember that every moment can be a prayer. Melting butter, scrambling eggs, lifting a fork to mouth, praising God.

Losing your temper and your dignity with someone you love, praising God. Balancing ecstasy with clear thinking, self control with self-abandon. Be still. Listen. Keep walking.

What a spectacular kingdom you have entered! Befriending the guards and taming the lions at the gates. Sliding through a crack in the doorway on your prayer rug. Crossing the moat between this world and that, walking on water if you have to, because this is your rightful place. That is your Beloved reclining in the innermost chamber, waiting for you, offering wine from a bottle with your crest on the label. Explore. Rest if you have to, but don't go to sleep. Head straight for his arms.

And when you have dismissed the serpents of vanity and greed, conquered the lizards of self importance, and lulled the monkey mind to sleep, your steps will be lighter. When you have given up everything to make a friend a cup of tea and tend her broken heart, stood up against the violation of innocent children and their fathers and mothers, made conscious choices to live simply and honour the earth, your steps will be lighter. When you have grown still on purpose while everything around you is asking for your chaos, you will find the doors between every room of this interior castle thrown open, the path home to your true love unobstructed after all.

[*The Interior Castle,* St Teresa of Avila tr by Mirabai Starr Rider, Random House, p. 2]

Why Pray This Prayer

I give five benefits below, but the compelling reason is that it works!

1. FREEDOM FROM FEAR: How many things make you fear? Darkness and terrors of the night; disease and malignant forces. But in the secret place fear is banished. "I sought the LORD and he delivered me from all my fears!"

2. JUSTICE: Thousands will fall at our side. The wicked will receive the reward for their deeds. So do not fret God is Just.

3. THE PROTECTION OF ANGELS: The angels of God will be on your side. Bodyguards of the highest order will watch over you.

4. PERSONAL VICTORY: God promises we will trample down every opposition and enemy, whether lion or serpent, organisation or gang. Sin cannot win. God's amazing grace is sufficient

5   PERSONAL SALVATION AND A FULL LIFE: Points to fulfilment on earth and a glory beyond this life.

Jesus Christ and Psalm 91

Consider the birth of Jesus when King Herod tried to deceive the Magi into revealing Jesus' whereabouts so he could kill him. Through a dream Jesus is delivered, *'Surely he will deliver me from the snare of the fowler' [v.3]*. The next crisis was the mass murder of the babies and

Joseph was warned to escape through a dream. *'A thousand shall fall around you' [v.7]*. We have many instances of Jesus spending time in prayer with God: as Mark 1 v35 puts it:

> Very early next morning, long before
> daylight, Jesus got up and left the house.
> He went out of town to a lonely place,
> where he prayed.

Remember when Jesus preached in his home town and people tried to throw him over a cliff: Jesus walked through the middle of the crowd and went on his way. The accounts of Jesus casting out demons or healing diseases, though they do not mention our psalm, do underline God's power to carry out the promises we will be studying. Jesus was under a continuous threat as the chief Priests, the teachers and the leaders of the people wanted to kill him but he was safe until his work was done. When after baptism the Holy Spirit descended on Jesus as a dove it was as though he was in God's feather nest.

Also Jesus is recorded as receiving direct angelic help of the sort offered in Psalm 91:

1. After the temptation in the wilderness [Matt 4:11]

2. At the Garden of Gethsemane [Luke 22:43f not included in all versions]

Finally, he famously refused to misuse the promises of Psalm 91 to test God. He warned apostles not to overvalue miraculous earthly protection over divine destiny [Luke 10:19-20].

Realistic warnings

Although some see the promises of the psalm as too absolute to be credible, the risks facing any who ignore the mind-set of this psalm are real enough:

1) Being EXPOSED to the law of the jungle: Jesus lamented over Jerusalem, "How often, I wanted to gather your children together as a hen gathers her brood under her wings, but you were not willing!" A few years later Jerusalem was ransacked by the Romans.

2) COMPLACENCY which means that we underestimate the enemy and his speed of attack and overestimate our capacity to respond. Alfred Hitchcock captured this when discussing the theme of his film *The Birds;* "If you like you can make it the theme of too much complacency in the world: that people are unaware that catastrophe surrounds us all." [Cameron Ian & Perkins V F: Interview with Alfred Hitchcock. Mocie 6/1/1963]

3) PRESUMPTION where rather than seeking guidance from God about our lives, we expect him to follow us into anything that suits us.

When To Pray The Promise

In the USA the emergency number is 911. Some Americans have therefore called the Psalm 'God's 911'. The Psalm has been given for us to use whenever we feel under threat, either personally or communally.

Bible prophecies talk of the 'last days' as the time between the Ascension and Jesus Christ's return. These will be times of violence and disaster. But in our generation 11 September 2001 will be remembered as a point in time when the world changed course and reality overstepped fiction and terrorism came close to becoming a declaration of war. Unfortunately there is no reason to believe this will turn out to be the last time that innocent lives are snuffed out, leaving dreams and hopes unfulfilled.

Use this any place there are threats, be it at the level of nation, county, city, town, neighbourhood, street corner, school, workplace or home.

Salvation through Psalm 91

1) Once a Jewish lady and her friends were praying for a man who was in his 91st year. They had agreed to pray Psalm 91 corresponding to his age everyday at 12.00. At the end of a Jewish Festival, she was due to go out but she was tired and her little child was playing around. The women decided to take a nap. This was at 11.50, ten minutes before the agreed time of prayer. Just before 12.00 using all her will power she got up to go to the

kitchen and pick up the prayer book. To her horror the kitchen was on fire and smoke billowing out. She grabbed her child and warned the neighbours who all managed to escape before the fire could kill someone. She couldn't help thinking that the God of Psalm 91 helped her while she was praying its promises for another.

2) Manila 1945: fighting block by block, the Japanese were moving downtown. Soon Manila the 'Pearl of the Orient' would be devastated. Located in the residential area was a small Protestant church, five or six blocks from downtown. That Sunday morning two friends attended the church. The church was filled with members and soldiers. It was communion Sunday and the pastor had chosen Psalm 91 as his Bible text. Everyone knelt at the altar to partake of the bread and the wine. The noise of the fighting was very loud. The artillery were shelling Japanese positions and a shell dropped nearby. The earth shook and dust from the ceiling came down. The whole congregation stayed in place and there was no panic and nothing happened. Two worshippers were struck at how appropriate the psalm was;

> He shall cover you with his feathers and under his wings you shall trust … a thousand shall fall at your side and ten thousand at your right hand: but it shall not come near you.

The service came to an end. The two came away believing that divine providence was caring for them and would care for them throughout this dark time they were passing through.

In fact Psalm 91 is often called *The Soldier's Psalm* because throughout history soldiers have prepared themselves for the dangers of the fight by reading Psalm 91.

But I would like to put forward one definite battlefield of terror: inside our own minds and spirits. God knew this and that is why he inspired the Psalmist to write. The banner of God's freedom is within you. 'For God has not given you a spirit of fear but of power, love and a sound mind.'

How This Prayer Works

Back to the priest who is speaking, "By praying Psalm 91, you put yourself into God's protection. Let me illustrate the point from Charles Wesley's Diaries."

It was Tuesday October 11th. I set out for London. In a mile's riding my horse fell lame. I sung the 91st Psalm, and put myself under divine protection. I had scarce ended, and turned the hut, on Shootover-Hill , when a man came up to me, and demanded my money, showing but not presenting, a pistol. I gave him my purse. He asked how much there was. 'About thirty shillings'. 'Have you no more?' 'I will see;' put my hand in my pocket, and gave him some half pence. He repeated the question, 'Have you no more?' I had thirty pounds in a private pocket; bade him search for himself; which he did not choose. He ordered me to dismount, which I did; but begged hard for my horse again, promising not to pursue him. He took my word and restored him. I rode gently on, praising God. My bags, and watch, and gold the robber was forced to leave me. By evening I reached Westminster.

Psalm 91 looks at how to overcome, how to get through life with all it throws at you and with all your mistakes. It addresses the great problem of how to face life with all the uncertainty and attendant problems and yet to get the victory: how to live your life instead of being mastered by it. It takes you on a real trip. So when you are staring eyeball to eyeball with troubles, it's no time for theory: these truths must kick in. The writer here is talking from experience. It is not theory. He has faced the battle and the problem of life. He has laid his head down on a pillow and slept like a child surrounded by his enemies. 'I laid me down and slept; I awakened and the LORD sustained me.'

He had learnt that confident trust in God and the troubles, afflictions physical, emotional, psychological and spiritual he faced could be overcome if 'God is your refuge and strength.' When he writes, 'He is my refuge and fortress my God in whom I trust' that it not just a promise, it is also a witness to specific past instances of finding help in times of danger.

By rehearsing this Psalm, you are believing God's promises regarding outcomes yet to happen, often quite imminent. As you pray on these situations, a confidence given from God will take over your anxiety and fear as you trust his word.

We must be in the place where God can depend on us to keep going until we see victory, never giving in on him, never knowing defeat, always making our stand by a living trust and gaining the victory. Trust is in itself a victory! Like the story about a Franco-British battle where some English soldiers had been taken prisoner including a drummer boy. Napoleon ordered him to sound a retreat. He said, "No ! I have never learned one."

It opens up actual help from God daily on our journey through life. For us this prayer puts the variety of threats we all face such as terrors, diseases, verbal intimidation etc before our imagination and they are overruled by God's promise of protection and deliverance. It creates a cry in our heart and a boldness in our soul. It establishes a confidence and point of view in a God who can and will act in our life on our behalf. We are finite, fallen and fallible, God is infinite, invincible and intimate. He will intervene on our behalf. He will show the error of terror.

The Traveller on a Dangerous Journey

The writer of this Psalm is not known. The possibility lies heavily with Moses or David as many incidents in their lives are reflected in Psalm 91.

The Traveller, whom you will be meeting regularly in the daily studies below, is in my imagination the great leader Moses, possibly seen through the eyes of the Psalmist (if the psalm was not composed by Moses). Whoever it was, one thing is sure, he made a practice of dwelling in the Secret Place. He was the sort of man who was not ignorant of life, having no doubt experienced luxury and want, leadership and slavery, security and crisis. The overarching fact is that the evils he has faced and overcome are the basis of his testimony. The confidence of how God has sustained him is what he recommends categorically. Moses was once a courtier in the most powerful empire in the world and now is wanted for murder. On the run, he has lived in the wilderness and worked as a shepherd. Now he has returned to his people. Looking around the Traveller can see the people worn down by the ordinary things of life, pretending to get by but only surviving. They bear the marks of exploitation and intimidation. The powers-that-be are preparing a last showdown.

The Traveller is restless and uncomfortable (a fish out of water). He has accepted the call and he is about to take a dangerous journey. He must lead his people to a better land. The way ahead lies through barren deserts – a long way out of the people's comfort zone. And the destination land is hostile, filled with dangers.

But at the outset he goes to the secret place and there talks to his God. This God assures him of his presence. He promises his help in all situations. The Traveller is so overjoyed he cries out to God in praise and affirmation.

The journey begins! Soon enough, they are pinned against the Red Sea in front of them and an army bearing down on them. He cries out to God! The sea is deep and they have no boats – they are cornered. Then God acts, in plain sight he splits the sea piling up the waters to the right and left, allowing the people to walk through. As the oncoming army follow on God reverses the miracle. "Behold with your eyes you will see the punishment of the wicked."

I believe that the Psalmist was inspired by the memory of the story of the Exodus and the wilderness wanderings as he composed this psalm – particularly the perceived presence of God in the cloud by day and the pillar of fire by night. In the verse-by-verse meditations that follow, I will seek out references to this well-known story that illustrate the points as well as looking for modern applications.

This Traveller's elixir was the initiative in seeking God in his secret place. This has resulted in a profound commitment from God. This God is resolved to answer any real life threats and is very sure none will prevail. He says, "I AM WHO I AM". Martial protection and power will sometimes be required, but beneath this is an intimacy and God speaks the last word to him of salvation.

We all from time to time embark on journeys which may start innocently enough until suddenly accident, crime or unfriendly actions ambush us. In this world, the fact is there are groups, organisations, gangs, individuals and forces, seen and unseen who want to impose their will on you and they will not disappear. Their aim is to expose you, individually and in community, to threats and entrapments designed to make you feel vulnerable. The consequence is that we can live our lives on the back foot of fear instead of the front foot of faith.

Psalm 91 does not seek to minimise the dangers but to face them down. As it is written,

> But the LORD will make a distinction between the livestock of Israel and the livestock of Egypt, so that nothing will die of all that belongs to the sons of Israel. And the LORD set a definite time, saying, "Tomorrow the LORD will do this thing in the land." So the LORD did this thing on the morrow, and all the livestock of Egypt died; but of the livestock of the sons of Israel, not one died.

There are times when God makes a distinction between his people and others. It means something to have God the Almighty on our side. This is what Israel learned under Moses, and the Psalmist is claiming here this sort of special treatment. That's why it makes sense to stay close to the will of God by meeting him often in the secret place.

OVERVIEW AND ANALYSIS

Psalm 91 NKJV

1 He who dwells in the secret place of the Most High shall abide under the shadow of the Almighty.

2 I will say of the LORD, "He is my refuge and my fortress; My God, in Him I will trust."

3 Surely He shall deliver you from the snare of the fowler and from the perilous pestilence.

4 He shall cover you with His feathers, and under His wings you shall take refuge; His truth shall be your shield and buckler.

5 You shall not be afraid of the terror by night, nor of the arrow that flies by day,

6 Nor of the pestilence that walks in darkness, nor of the destruction that lays waste at noonday.

7 A thousand may fall at your side, and ten thousand at your right hand; but it shall not come near you.

8 Only with your eyes shall you look, and see the reward of the wicked.

9 Because you have made the LORD, who is my refuge, even the Most High, your dwelling place,

10 No evil shall befall you, nor shall any plague
    come near your dwelling;
11 For He shall give His angels charge over you,
    to keep you in all your ways.
12 In their hands they shall bear you up,
    lest you dash your foot against a stone.
13 You shall tread upon the lion and the cobra,
    the young lion and the serpent you shall
    trample underfoot.
14 "Because he has set his love upon Me, therefore
    I will deliver him; I will set him on high,
    because he has known My name.
15 He shall call upon Me, and I will answer him;
    I will be with him in trouble; I will deliver him
    and honor him.
16 With long life I will satisfy him,
    and show him My salvation."

'Psalm' is Greek for song but of course the Bible
Book of Psalms was composed in Hebrew –
their word is 'tehillim', praises sung. Here are
150 songs presented in five books, with the 91st
in book 4 , one of the set of psalms 90-106 from a
royal collection, perhaps for the new year. It is a
Royal Psalm of Trust where a Court Poet or
Prophet would have chanted this Psalm to the
King: the message is that the ruler would be
safe if he will only place all his hope and confidence in God.

Big Picture

Trust characterises the whole Psalm, entrusting
oneself to God like a child. The lesson to be

learnt is that confidence in God in the midst of trouble and peril is the privilege of those who regularly seek him in the secret place. God promises, 'He who believe in me will not be disappointed.' Trust leads on to the theme of refuge, God's active presence in the face of danger: 'No weapon formed against me will prosper.'

The Writer

Psalm 91 is without title and we have no means of ascertaining either the name of its writer or the date of its composition with certainty. In the Septuagint it is ascribed to David. Ancient rabbis assigned the psalm to Moses, whose name is on Psalm 90, on the theory that unassigned psalms implied there was no change of author from the previous. Also they felt that one verse was drawn from the Passover night when the destroying angel passed through Egypt while the faithful and obedient Israelis were sheltered by God through the blood of the lamb or goat. The ascription to David is based on the occasion of the pestilence which was inflicted upon the people as a punishment of his sin in numbering them [2 Samuel 24]. Some believe it maybe a dialogue between David and Solomon. Similarities with [Job 5:19-24] have led proposals to link it with wisdom writings, but Job itself may have been influenced by the Psalm's form. In truth, the text itself does not allow a firm conclusion on the identity of its inspired author or the occasion of composition.

Relationship to other Psalms

Two Psalms 120 & 3 have significant overlap in terms of subject-matter with our chosen one carrying a similar message of safety arising out of abiding in the presence of God. The key lesson is always that in life you will not be exempt from troubles, difficulties and trials: God's security is not necessarily from them but in them. The message of the Bible is clear that for the faithful there is something greater than the absence of pain, opposition or trial. The theme of closeness to God as the ultimate place of refuge is central.

Psalm 91 is also naturally positioned between Psalm 90 and Psalm 92 in section 4 of the Book of Psalms. The relationship between 90 and 91 is established by the occurrence of the relatively rare word 'dwelling place'.

> Lord you have been our dwelling place...
> [Psalm 90:1]

> ... and the Most High your dwelling
> place. [Psalm 91:9]

Even more striking is that two of the concluding petitions of Ps 90:13-17 are explicitly answered in Ps 91:16 where GOD promises to satisfy:

> O satisfy us with your mercy and loving kindness in the morning, that we may rejoice and be glad all our days [Ps 90:14]

> With long life will I satisfy him and show him my salvation [Ps 91:16].

The promise of satisfaction with 'length of days' is particularly apt after Psalm 90 and its focus on human transience, brevity and mortality. Psalm 90 stresses that there is no chance for humans apart from God given the brevity of life. Psalm 90 seems to be pleading for God to satisfy us / make us glad; i.e. let your work be seen. Psalm 91 seems to answer this by affirming God will satisfy them no matter what dangers are around. Here are some more contrasts and answers:

Psalm 90	Psalm 91
Man is withering away beneath God's anger against sin.	Here is one who is able to tread the lion and adder under his feet.
God is Sovereign.	God is tender and full of loving-kindness.
The brevity of human life	Long life and salvation found in God
A soul full of trouble and fear	A soul no longer in fear but trusting in God

Structure of Psalm

The natural way to grasp the sequence of thought is to note the three changes of viewpoint: first-person statements by the Psalmist to God [vs 1,2]; third-person pictures and illustrations adduced by the Psalmist; then strikingly the psalm ends with I-statements in the name of God himself.

Developing these three sections:

1. Assurance of the security of the believer due to God's presence and protection [verses 1,2]. This is faith's prospectus to the one who seeks God in his temple.

2. Insurance with comprehensive protection covering every kind of threat, trial and trouble in life and every weapon, tactic and attack [vv 3-13]. Protection from dangers encountered on the way. This is faith's experience.

3. Reassurance of God's salvation and love [vv 14-end] This is faith's guarantee.

The Psalmist has been inspired to use emphatic personal pronouns of God (as in "I will be with you in troubles"): for a Hebrew to dare to speak in the 1st person when this is so close to the revealed name of God reflects the author's assurance that he worships a God who reveals himself. The intensity of God's love is hard to convey in English. One can illustrate the difference by comparing it to a small garden fountain of love versus Niagara Falls. The Psalmist has also varied the names he uses for God: The MOST HIGH (= more important than anyone else), ALMIGHTY (= more powerful than anything else), THE LORD (= never dies, eternal). The nuances of meaning will be dealt with in the verse-by-verse section below, but the variety of names underlines that God is too great to be captured in just one name, which increases the confidence we can have in Him.

Another way to look at the Psalm is to expand the reference in verse 4 ("shield and buckler) to imagine God's protection as different kinds of shield:

The natural shield:

> God knows that all life needs protection; that is why he has given five senses which warn of danger, an endocrine system to condition us to fight or flee as well as an immune system to ward off germs. The Psalmist creates a need by listing various crises that can befall anyone.

The individual shield:

> But nature is not always enough: wars make body bags and sparrows end up in nets! So 'you' becomes personal and emphatic! "To you it will not draw"; "Keep you in all your ways"; God is with you, a super bodyguard – but 'you' are also responsible to seek out his provision.

The miraculous shield:

> Invisible Angels provide protection along your way. You are protected far more than statistics would lead you to expect.

Finally, the content can be analysed as eight promises from The Lord which cover initial saving action (rescue) right through to fully enjoyed salvation and cover all intervening needs (New Century Bible p546).

1. *Security*

2. *Rescue*

3. *Serenity*

4. *Vindication*

5. *Supernatural guard*

6. *Listening presence*

7. *Honour / favour*

8. *Eternal life*

The eight promises depend on the basic conditions of dwelling in the secret place [v1 repeated in v9]. Active cooperation with God is no doubt also required:–

1. to cease from panic [v5-6]

2. to cling to God in love [v14]

3. to know His name [v14]

4. to pray [v15].

The first word of the psalm was an expression of human trust, and the Psalmist reserves the last word for God by ending the psalm in God's word of promise. God is the ultimate ground of our confidence, security and hope.

APPLICATIONS

During a period of peril, tribulation and despair Euthanases, the fourth century Bishop of Alexandria, Egypt, offered this advice to Marcellinus, younger, less experienced Bishop; "If you desire to establish yourself and others in devotion, to know what confidence is to be reposed in God, and what makes the mind fearless, you will praise God by reciting the 91st Psalm."

The powerful thing about Psalm 91 is that each one can apply it to their life taking account of their personal pressures.

Generally the application is for anyone under threat or stress. There is this flexibility as W Brueggemann points out; 'This remarkable psalm speaks with great specificity, and yet with a kind of porousness, so the language is enormously open to each one's particular experience.' So there is a flexibility in how to use and apply it.

APPLICATION : traditional

The psalm is entirely general in application. It is of great service to the traveller and all who are exposed to dangers both seen and unseen. It addresses the insecurity of life and health and the fear of malignant unseen powers by which men can be oppressed. But over and against them is set the security of those who trust in the Almighty. In fact Psalm 91 has been known as the Soldier's Prayer. For centuries, soldiers facing hazards of combat have popularly considered Psalm 91 as their shield of protection. Whether its arrows or bullets, missiles, rocks or rockets, biological weapons or enemy gas getting close to their targets, Warriors are suddenly confronted with their own vulnerability and mortality.

When surrounded by these real and present dangers, the love, protection and salvation proclaimed in Psalm 91 is a source of comfort for those in these situations and extends to the soldiers a sense of the loving presence of Almighty God. Many Jewish soldiers going into battle pray Psalm 91.

Its wording has made it a traditional night prayer. Rabbi Yehoshua Ben Levi recited Psalm 91 of Tehillim before retiring at night to protect himself against the dangers of the night. He did this as a preventative.

Believers Jewish and Christian

God can miraculously deliver from physical crises. The immense practicality of this psalm is that everyone sees with foresight the possibility of numberless evils and dangers which no prudence, strength, courage, calculation of our own can possibly deal with. Set against this uncertainty is the Fortress of the Most High.

Psalm 91 is one of the Psalms recited in traditional Jewish funerals. At the cemetery another custom is to stop – seven times – as the coffin is carried to the grave-and to recite Psalm 91. Once the coffin is lowered into the grave, family and close friends cover the coffin with a few handfuls of dirt. Then the Rabbi repeats Psalm 91 and El Maleh Rachamim.

Then there is Spiritual Warfare: Psalm 91 is effective in countering curses and spells. A traditional Jewish application is against demons, for the Jews believed that their enemies attacked them by curses (ill will, hate) and magic causing drought, pestilence and harm. Psalm 91 was used to implore God's protection and counter-action.

The curative and protective power of Psalm 91 is mentioned several times in the Talmud. In the exile to Babylon, the Jews were cast into a culture where magic and spiritism was used. From this unsavoury morass, it is instructive to see the Jews use this prayer at counter-charm services. By implication the Psalmist opposes superstitious practices such as putting trust in amulets, guardian angels, good luck charms. The only place to generate security is in the secret place of the LORD.

Some people have seen in it the framework of a Babylonian counter charm, purified by sincere belief. It opens up four names of God – The Most High, the Almighty, the LORD and God and proclaims (which was a common

Jewish way of making a prayer for an urgent need) that God will preserve them from the trap and snares, from any terrifying words of destruction that are unleashed by magic which can undermine a person as he anticipates how a curse may overpower his human resources.

.

APPLICATION *more unusual*

A doctor in USA distributes Psalm 91 to patients who are emotionally or psychologically disturbed. This doctor advocates trust in God as being a way of helping people with mental illness.

The words of the Psalm strike the special chord for those with schizophrenia. Those with schizophrenia, like the Psalmist, feel overwhelmed by the terror at night, the various arrows that fly by day and the pestilence that stalks in the darkness. The biochemical disorder affects the pathways of the brain down which messages travel. These messages may not get through or only do so in a distorted manner. Schizophrenia affects the ability to correctly interpret the outside world. It also affects an individual's ability to actively engage with the outside world, and his ability to focus attention on problem solving. The Psalmist gives the assurance that the shelter of the most high will act as a shield against dark forces

There is also the potential for misapplication of the psalm to justify certain attention-seeking behaviours. Did you know that Psalm 91 is the only scripture spoken by God, Jesus Christ and the Devil? As we can see, the latter misquotes it on purpose.

The Jewish Prayer book suggest that this prayer is meant to be read before going to bed. John Stott comments "only the children of God who are living in the will of God in expectation of God's protection." If we confess our sins he is faithful and just and will forgive our sins and cleanse us from unrighteousness.

OUR 91-SECOND 91-DAY PROPOSAL

'Be prepared' is the motto of the scouting movement. None of us knows when or where a crisis will hit so the best way to be ready is to have something worked out in advance.

The starting point is that you are open to the idea that God lovingly wants all his people to live without dread and that true security is in his gift. We suggest that you burn into your heart the teaching of this psalm, and even learn the verses by heart.

The end point? In Revelation 15:3, the saved are singing the 'song of Moses': this may refer to Exodus 15 (though Psalm 90 would be appropriate in connection with the harvest of the Earth): the hint is that singing psalms is a foretaste of Heaven!

The Plan

For the next 91 days make the 91st Psalm your prayer.

Step 1:   Every day pray the 91st Psalm –
          taking (we like to think) about 91
          seconds. Choose your favourite
          version and gradually you will learn

it. Ideally go to a quiet place and look to God who has said, "Come near to me and I will come near to you."

Step 2: Read the daily meditations as this will deepen your understanding of the Psalm; what is understood is easier to memorise and hopefully some of the stories will also aid recall.

Step 3: See if you can enjoy and get acquainted with some musical version (modern, chanted or whatever). Get a CD or an MP3 file and sing along with it.

Step 4: Do this for 30 days as your main daily meditation and then go back over the ground a second and a third time (possibly as a subsidiary) until the 90th day. On the 91st you can celebrate your milestone.

Step 5: Keep a journal of God's help and protection. You may wish to tell others of any escapes you experience at info@terror-rest.net.

Step 6: Adapt the 91st Psalm to your own situation using words of your own in the framework of Psalm 91 (some examples in appendix)

Step 7:   Thank God for his greatness and
            help.

Year Challenge!

The Year challenge is that you can break down
the year into 4 quarters of 91 days = 364 days!!
  On the 365th day you can celebrate !

Meditations

Below are thirty meditations which will help
you memorize the Psalm and make it your
own. We have based these on the New King
James Version of the text, not on the basis of
accuracy but rather of familiarity and
learnability. You can however choose the
version you prefer and you will find that the
website www.terror-rest.net guides you to a
wide variety of versions (some unusual).

  Each one has an illustrative or provocative
story taken from real life; then I have imagined
a possible application or reference of the psalm
in the story of the Exodus. Finally some commentary on the text, and a prayer.

  Some of the stories are hard to believe, even
controversial. They should be seen as pointers
to what could happen *but not Scriptural truth!*
As author I do believe the ones I have included,
but they are second-hand experiences for me:
Ultimately this is something that I am inviting
you to ask yourself: how much do you believe
God's promises? In addition, just as in other
Scriptures, you may in each daily portion wish
to look out for:-

- a warning for you;

- a promise to claim;

- an example to follow;

- a command or rule to obey;

- a consciousness of error past or present that you must admit and put right;

- some word of encouragement;

- some reason to praise and thank God.

Wherever there's a spiritual challenge, our hearts have a way of subtly reinterpreting it as an opportunity for boastfulness. It is worth remembering Jesus Christ's advice on prayer: "Go into your room close the door and pray to your father in secret." Then this place becomes your meeting place with God.

If your situation is too fraught to find an island of peace, however, it is fine to speak to God at any time in your heart.

Qualification

The stories given in the meditations are mostly success stories. Towards the end of Chapter 11 in the book of Hebrews, where the Old Testament victories through faith are celebrated, the writer makes it clear that faith also helped those who faced apparent defeat – torture, mocking, imprisonment, death, exile [Heb

11:35ff]. We cannot know why some are called to great and famous victories while others are called to witness to their faith through suffering.

But we get a hint in the very next chapter of Epistle to the Hebrews: the writer turns his thoughts to Christ, who "for the joy that was set before him endured the cross, despising the shame" [Heb 12:2 RSV]. It is so clear that Jesus could have summoned an army of angels to rescue him from the cross; this was indeed the final taunt even as he hung at Calvary ["He saved others, himself he could not save"]. This was a last temptation that had to be refused.

Psalm 90 has reminded us all of our mortality: 'return to dust O children of men'. Death is the consequence of sin entering the world, and Jesus had not only to purchase an atonement for our sins in the legal sphere but also to demonstrate that the physical consequence of sin, namely Death, had been beaten.

I do not wish to spiritualise the promises of Psalm 91: they include the physical, and we can see that Jesus' death and resurrection actually makes the promises more credible. Sometimes, however, Christians face more than one threat: one a very real physical one and on the other a serious moral temptation (eg coveting success at any price, bowing to an idol, …). Sometimes they can only be saved from the latter by paying the price of the former. This can be the 'snare of the fowler'…

DAY 1:   THE SAFEST PLACE
           IN THE WORLD

*V1 He who dwells in the secret place of
the Most High*

Story

On July 7th, 2005 Sandy Kirkwood was in a
prayer meeting at his local Church and had his
phone switched off to avoid interruptions. He
was not to know that at that precise time four
terrorists bombs were to change London life
forever. He writes:

> "As the Railway Chaplain for the West
> Midlands and the British Transport
> Police, I have grown used to bad news,
> fatalities and accidents, but none of that
> prepared me for the news I received from
> the Mission Director. 'Sandy; make your
> way into Birmingham Transport Police
> Headquarters as quick as you can, there's
> been bombs in the stations in London.'

> "I'd seen what a bomb could do in my
> twenty two years with the Armed Forces,
> and I found myself thinking *I don't want
> this....I don't want to go there* Doubts
> flooded my mind, *What can I do?....Will I
> be able to cope....*would I be up to showing
> the Love of the Father in the midst of the
> carnage I knew to expect?

> "On the site my whole attitude was quite
> simply "Just get on and do it". And I

found, as I always knew but often forget that, 'He who dwells in the shelter of the Most High will abide in the shadow of the Almighty' (Ps.91:1)

"Even in times of the greatest challenges Father never removes our covering and I rediscovered that week in London that His strength is always available. The same Scripture that sustained many soldiers in combat situations, some of whom I know personally, sustained me in my own moment of need."

Traveller's Tale

He was a 120 year old and strong as an ox, with eyesight still sharp as an eagle's; from the mountaintop he could look across the River Jordan and see the Promised Land. He remembered how it started 40 years ago in the wilderness when he was drawn into a private meeting with God and called for this extraordinary adventure.

He looked back over all the subsequent meetings with God both in his nomad's tent and on mountain tops. The key to his success was having the Almighty shadowing and helping him with whatever he faced. But the whole enterprise stemmed upon meeting God regularly in his secret place. Once this condition was met the benefits fell together like a line of dominos.

Word-by-word

HE WHO:	everyone or any one – No membership or qualifications needed. God invites all to choose to live close to him.
DWELLS:	is a reflective word meaning voluntary taking up residence or sitting in an active sense.
IN THE SECRET PLACE:	literally 'In the hidden place.' Hidden from enemies, rather than hard to find. There is also an idea of protection: it's not that the enemy does not know where it is, but that he cannot pierce through to it.
OF	Our hideaway is not private, ultimately it belongs to God himself.

THE MOST HIGH:	Elyon: God has an elevated position far higher than the highest spy satellites that are so useful in modern warfare. He is far superior to the idols of Canaan or Egypt.

Other versions

- We live within the shadow of the Almighty (LB);
- Whoever goes to the Lord for safety (GN);
- You who sit down in the High God's presence (TM);
- … The shelter of the most High (ESV).

Prayer

Lord Jesus, you taught your apostles to abide in you like the branches in a vine. I come now into your special place of quiet rest, where sin and insecurity cannot reach me. I desire a heart-to-heart communion with you more than anything else.

DAY 2: THE SHADOW

*V1 Shall abide under the shadow
of the Almighty*

Story

Jack McKee, Pastor of the New Life Fellowship Northern Ireland: "If ever Psalm 91 had any real significance for me personally, and for those with whom we work and have fellowship, it was surely during the year 2000. The year started well; then a darkness descended destroying families and homes.

"It was during this period that the first 8 verses of Psalm 91 took on a role of immediate significance for the New Life Fellowship. God was telling us that as we would dwell in the shelter of the Most High, we would also rest in the Shadow of the Almighty and not fear the terror of the night or the arrow that flies by day."

On Saturday 19th August 2000 feuds around the Shankhill area erupted into violence. 7 people were shot, 40 families put out of their homes. Fear gripped the community.

Jack's church responded by reaching out to the community through a peace walk, helping people to move home through the night. The youth club became a half-way house for people's furniture. During the darkest hours groups from the church befriended the frightened residents. Even the paratroopers patrolling the area were impressed by the church's sensitivity and courage. They told the church that if any of their groups got into difficulties they should approach any of the paratroop units.

Jack said, "However, our hiding place and our resting place was not the British army but under the Shadow of the Almighty. 'In God we trust' is not a religious or national statement but a statement of faith that has been tried and tested. For as Paul said, 'Greater is he that is in us than he that is in the world'."

Traveller's Tale

Into the shadowlands of the wilderness the Traveller and his people go. He asserts they are living under the shadow of the Almighty which is greater than the shadow of enemies, demons and natural threats, terrors and disease. The cloud of the Almighty that leads them throws back a shadow that covers them during the day. The Pillar of Fire, which would otherwise reveal their whereabouts to enemies, is a flaming threat and searchlight against anyone intending an attack in the night. Even though the Traveller may not understand how God will work things out. He takes his stand on this verse and looks to God to overrule their lives and his presence to overshadow their whole journey through life. Imagine the

Shadow of the Almighty covering you as you go about your daily business.

Word-by-word

SHALL ABIDE:	very similar to dwell; the nuance is the difference between the place where you live and the lodging or resting place where you are going to pass your nights. We all need to sleep, and yet that is when we are most vulnerable and where protection counts most.
UNDER THE SHADOW:	The literal 'shadow' almost certainly means the defence of the Almighty. It is dangerous to sleep both in the beating radiation of the full desert sun and at night. The protection we need is not some gizmo or commodity but the wisdom and strength of a trustworthy protector. Like a chick needs the protection of a mother-bird.

OF THE ALMIGHTY:	Shaddai: is a name indicating the above-and-beyond-ness of God from those things that threaten. But he is not so far removed that he cannot or will not act powerfully. He can do anything. "Cast all your cares on the LORD for He careth for you."

Other versions

- Sheltered by the God who is above all gods (LB);
- Whoever remains under the protection of the Almighty (GN);
- Spend the night in Shaddai's shadow (TM).

Prayer

Lord Almighty I rest beneath the shade of your protecting wings. In the stillness of your presence my griefs expire, my troubles cease; My heart wants to sing: "Under the shadow of thy throne, your saints have dwelt secure; sufficient is your arm alone, and our defence is sure."

DAY 3 :   THE CASTLE

V2a I will say of the LORD, he is my refuge and my fortress

Story

In 1941 the US entered World War 2 and Jimmy Stewart, the American actor, enlisted in the Army Air Corps. His dad Alex, a veteran of the Spanish American War, choked for words, sent a letter to be read en route.

"My dear boy. Soon after you read this letter, you will be on your way to the worst sorts of danger. Jim, I'm banking on the enclosed copy of the 91st Psalm. The thing that takes the place of fear and worry is the promise of these words. I am staking my faith in these words. I feel that God will lead you through this mad experience..."

Jimmy Stewart returned home a decorated war hero; but more than that, he was prepared to go on record praising and thanking God: as he told his father, "What a promise for an airman. I placed in his hands the squadron I would be leading and as the Psalm promised, I felt myself borne up."

Traveller's Tale

From the mountain top The Traveller looked into the valley. There was the camp it was a good camp he thought. It was guarded well. Joshua and Caleb had learnt well he thought. but then he looked over to the fortified cities of Canaan; for a moment he thought: if they lose a battle they can always run to the next citadel. But as a wandering people, if we lose any battle we only have the wide-open desert to run to.

But he knew that their real security and safety came from the LORD alone. He is the refuge and fortress that they cannot have physically. Others may say their wealth is their refuge, their house, their family, their degrees, their looks or their success. Goethe puts the Psalmist's words in briefest compass:

"Wer Gott vertraut, ist schon auferbaut" (He who trusts God is already built up).

Word-by-word

I WILL SAY:	confidence often comes from verbalising a thought. It also strengthens faith to risk speaking out. The confidence expressed here is one of the principal themes of this psalm.

OF THE LORD:	using the name YHWH, the Living God, the covenant God, the God who cannot lie. The name which later became almost too holy to pronounce.
HE IS MY REFUGE:	this is quite a claim: the infinite-personal God is a refuge even for my problems which are so small in the greater scheme of things.
AND FORTRESS:	refuge has some of the idea of legal right whereas fortress speaks of physical solidity.

Other Versions

- This I declare, that he alone is my refuge, my place of safety (LB);
- Can say to him "You are my defender and protector" (GN);
- Say this: "GOD, you're my refuge. I trust in you and I'm safe" (TM).

Prayer

Lord, my rock and fortress. Lead me and guide me so that your name may be honoured.

> Be thou my breastplate,
> my sword for the fight;

be thou my armour,
be thou my true might;
be thou my soul's shelter,
be thou my strong tower:
O raise thou me heavenward,
great power of my power.

DAY 4: THE CONFIDENCE

V2b My God in Him will I trust

Story

If you hold up the American dollar bill you will see it says, 'In God we trust'. But words are sometimes cheap when it comes to issues of trust.

Blondin was a world tightrope walker and acrobat who stretched a wire right across the Niagara Falls from Canada to America. He proceeded to walk across that wire with a long balancing pole. He crossed the thundering waters a second time carrying nothing in his hands at all. For the third crossing he pushed a wheelbarrow over that thin wire, returning with it loaded with potatoes. He was applauded in both countries and a host of reporters pressed on him to do it again. The crowds loved it, and voiced their admiration. He turned to the crowd and said,

"Do you believe that I could put a man in this wheelbarrow and take him across safely?"

One fellow said, "Yes, yes I believe that you can do it." Blondin replied, "OK, jump in!"

Blondin crossed Niagara with him. So it is with God, you are trusting your life to someone else – God Almighty.

Traveller's Tale

Now The Traveller thinks back again to the occasion of his call at the Burning Bush. God asked him to do the impossible, and added solemn promises of success: "I will bring you up out of the affliction of Egypt" [Exodus 3:17]. Moses had to believe enough to act on the call. So trust is often a two-way street: as we trust God, he entrusts greater missions and authority to us. He has decided that men and women should spread his Gospel rather than doing it all himself.

Word-by-word

MY GOD, IN HIM:	here is a personal address to a God who is accessible and available.
WILL I:	this is not just a persuasion about the future; speaking out such words can actually constitute the trust.
TRUST:	who is trustworthy? Being trusted is one of the most treasured political assets, though the Psalmist warns elsewhere "Put not your trust in princes nor in any child of man..."

Other versions

- He is my God, and I am trusting him (LB);
- You are my God, in you I trust (GN);
- My God, in whom I trust (ESV);
- My God, I will confide in him (JN Darby).

Prayer

My God in whom I trust, I have been disappointed both by my own attempted solutions and by the mixed motives of my human friends. You are my ultimate hope of safety; remind me to stay close to you at all times. And make me a trustworthy agent of Jesus Christ.

DAY 5:   THE DELIVERANCE

*V3 Surely he shall deliver you from the
snare of the fowler*

Story

Is the 'War on Terror' a trap? Was the intention of the 9/11 attacks to provoke the West to retaliate in order to turn us into legitimate targets? In the 1950s the Cold War also felt like a trap with its 'mutually assured destruction'.

At that time, a 79-year-old preacher in England known as 'Owd John' got up days after the British Prime Minister had given a solemn speech about the Hydrogen Bomb. The preacher thumped his Bible and said "If the Government stayed at home and read the good book, they'd find the answer had been there all the time … read Psalm 91 for yourselves."

The God who kept us through such crises as Berlin and Cuba can keep us through the war on terror even if there are traps set along our way … IF we abide in Him.

Traveller's Tale

The Traveller watches some young men try to capture birds: they have a net at the end of a hedge, and stones are thrown into the hedge. These stones don't hurt the birds, but the birds are frightened by the harmless noise and in their haste to escape are entangled in the nets.

Moses smiled and remembered how Balaam at Baalpeor tried to snare his people: first he was constrained by the Spirit to prophesy blessings instead of curses; then the Moabites and Midianites tried the 'honey trap' of sex, then social relationships followed by idol worship in order to undermine the abiding in God that was Israel's strength [Num 24-5].

It seems bigoted and unreasonable not to want to share society with unbelievers, but often it is easier not to go at all than to meet up and avoid going further than initially intended.

Word-by-word

SURELY:	emphatic exclamation, the Psalmist makes a beautiful apostrophe to the godly person he has been describing.
HE SHALL DELIVER YOU:	it may mean that God will frustrate the whole scheme, or it may involve you first being caught and then set free before the hunter can finish you off.

FROM THE SNARE:	the spring-net which normally is set to catch birds. The point is to first lead the quarry towards the trap and then to spring it before they can see it. There is often some sort of bait.
OF THE FOWLER:	a poacher, perhaps, who does not even have the right to hunt. Though even a legitimate hunter is bad news for the birds!

Other versions

- For he rescues me from every trap (LB);
- That's right—he rescues you from hidden traps (TM);
- For it is He who delivers you from the snare of the trapper (NASV).

Prayer

O God, you are the author of peace and lover of unity, in knowledge of whom stands our eternal life, whose service is perfect freedom. Defend us your humble servants in all assaults from our enemies, devices of the devil and all dangerous maladies; that we, surely trusting in your defence, may not fear the power of any adversaries, through the might of Jesus Christ our Lord.

DAY 6: DELIVERANCE FROM HARSH CURSES

V3b And from the perilous pestilence

Story

An insight from Spurgeon: when a hunter fails to trap a bird in his nets, his next move is often to employ a hawk: so similarly if Satan fails to tempt someone into flagrant sin, he sometimes arranges a 'Hawk' of slander. Spurgeon goes on to mention a fellow minister who was slandered, took the person to court, won the case, and had the papers duly publish an apology. The result? Many of the public who only learned of the allegations through the retraction, started believing the slander.

The solution? When slandered, don't try to 'set the record straight', just try to fly above it. For just as a hawk can only swoop down on prey when it starts above it, so we are less vulnerable if we refuse to come down to the level of trading allegations: King David in the Bible at a difficult moment was prepared to allow Shimei to speak badly of him: "If the LORD has given him commandment to curse, let him curse". When Jesus was reviled he did not answer back.

Traveller's Tale

The Traveller now thinks back to the plagues of Egypt: the wonderful way that these had targeted the Egyptians but left the children of Israel free. And then in the desert, it was because of the disobedience and grumbling of some of his own people that plagues were sent by way of a punishment. To think these had previously been the beneficiaries of God's former deliverances! A mystery indeed.

Word-by-word

AND FROM THE PERILOUS:	means deadly, destructive, fatal. (Heb:*havvah:*- one who eagerly covets, perverse thing, very wicked). Emphatic. Possibly hinting that the threat cannot be countered by human agencies.
PESTILENCE:	any scourge: in the pre-scientific world, people believed that accidents and epidemics were often either the result of pagan curses or were a punishment from God.

PESTILENCE (2):	many people believe that blind 'luck' is what decides whether one person recovers from disease or escapes some headline disaster. the believer believes that providence trumps luck every time.

Other Versions

- And protects you from the fatal plague (LB);
- And from all deadly diseases (GN);
- Shields you from deadly hazards (TM);
- From the deadly pestilence (ESV, NASB).

Prayer

Good Lord, you hold the destiny of each one of us in your hands. Help us to stand firm against the evil and slanderous harsh word, direct traps and indirect manoeuvres that are used against us; and thank you for all the times you delivered us from the same.

DAY 7:   THE COVERING

V4 He shall cover you with his feathers

Story

After a fire in Yellowstone National Park, Forest Rangers began their trek up a mountain to assess the inferno's damage. One Ranger found a bird literally petrified in ashes, perched statuesquely on the ground at the base of the tree, somewhat sickened by the eerie sight, he knocked the bird with a stick. When he struck it three tiny chicks scurried from under their dead mother's wings. The loving mother keenly aware of the impending disaster, had carried her offspring to the base of the tree and had gathered them under her wings, instinctively knowing toxic smoke would rise. She could have flown to safety but refused to abandon her babies. When the blaze arrived and the heat scorched her body she remained steadfast. Because she had been willing to die, those under the cover of her wings would live.

Traveller's Tale

The Traveller thinks back to Passover night – the night that the angel of death attacked the Egyptian firstborn. The homes of the Israelites were protected by the blood of the sacrificed lambs painted on the door frame. The death of all those lambs provided the covering for his people.

Word-by-word

HE WILL COVER:	to fence in, to cover, to defend: Although God is 'He' the act is typically a maternal one.
YOU:	singular; God tailors his help to your crisis.
WITH HIS FEATHERS:	although feathers are mostly for flying and looking beautiful, a mother-bird would rather risk losing some or getting them soiled than letting her chicks suffer risk.

Other Versions

- He will shield you with his wings! (LB)
- His huge outstretched arms protect you (TM)
- … with his pinions (ESV, NASB)

Prayer

Father Almighty, I bow before you and worship at your throne, you are my refuge and strength. Cover me with your feathers in the days of battle, attack and storm. Keep me safe under the shadow of the Almighty.

DAY 8:   THE WINGS

*V4a And under his wings you shall take
refuge*

Story

An artist's rendering of the scene of the returning prodigal son as described by Henri
Nouwen: "There is the great red cloak. With its
warm colour and its arch-like shape, it offers a
welcome place where it is good to be. At first,
the cloak covering the bent body of the father
looked to me like a tent inviting the tired traveller to find some rest. But as I went on gazing at
the red cloak, another image, stronger than that
of a tent came to me. The sheltering wings of
the mother bird. They reminded me of Jesus'
words about God's maternal love.

Day and night God holds me safe, as a hen
holds her chicks secure under her wings. Seen
more than that of a tent, the image of a vigilant
mother bird's wings expresses the safety that
God offers his children. They express care, protection, a place to rest and feel safe.

Every time I look at the tent – like looking at
Rembrandt's painting, I sense the motherly
quality of God's love and my heart begins to
sing in words inspired by the Psalmist…."

Traveller's Tale

One of the hardest moments for Moses was the aftermath of the golden calf episode: God was saying that from now on he would send an angel to drive out the pagan people from the promised land but his presence would no longer travel with them [Ex 33::1-17]. This was interpreted as very bad news by Moses: because, before when he went to the tabernacle to pray, the pillar of cloud had visibly joined him in the same 'secret place'. This was where Moses could count on to retreat when the responsibilities of leadership were too great. but if God no longer left him a bolt hole, then his task was superhuman.

Word-by-word

AND UNDER HIS WINGS:	a typical antiphon of Hebrew verse, where a point is repeated with a slightly different emphasis.
YOU SHALL TAKE REFUGE:	or 'you may seek refuge' (NASB). The initiative is in ourselves and our feelings of insecurity. God takes the initiative to help us in times of objective danger. But we can flee to him when we have a subjective need.

Other Versions

- Under them you're perfectly safe (TM);
- And under His wings you may seek refuge (NASB).

Prayer

Father you know that I need a bolt-hole for those moments when the pressures of the world just seem to crowd in. Thank you for never testing me beyond my strength.

> Other refuge have I none,
> hangs my helpless soul on you;
> leave, ah, leave me not alone,
> still support and comfort me.

DAY 9: THE ULTIMATE SHIELD

V4b His truth shall be your shield and buckler

Story

In the middle of a drawn out war against terrorists, military Christians in Sri Lanka continue to meet regularly for prayer and encouragement. During one of those meetings, when many MCF members were facing serious discouragement, God began proclaiming his presence in a powerful way through the reading of Psalm 91 (frequently called The Soldier's Psalm). Shortly after, Christian soldiers began wearing laminated copies of Psalm 91 around their necks. This practice began spreading to some non-Christians as well.

Within a short time miraculous stories began spreading through the troops about how those soldiers who prayed Psalm 91 were spared from harm and death. As one party of soldiers prepared to sweep a newly-taken road for mines, they stopped and prayed Psalm 91 together. Later, some distance away from the camp, a blast suddenly went off right in front of a soldier. Bushes and shrubs around him were flattened, but the soldier remained unharmed.

Flabbergasted, he began running back to the camp shouting, "Nothing happened to me! Nothing happened to me! Nothing happened to me!" A sergeant-major calmed him down and then heard the soldier's story: he had been sweeping for mines when there was a mighty explosion right in front of him. The soldier saw a sheet of light go up like a wall between him and the point of the explosion, and nothing penetrated that wall around him. The soldier attributed his escape from sure death to the God of Psalm 91. As one Sri Lankan Officer writes, "Faith begets miracles, for they are an acceptance of God's unique involvement with his creation."

Traveller's Tale

Then there was the fight with the Amalekites [Ex 17]. Joshua was leading the fighting and Moses was overlooking the plain grasping his rod. As long as Moses held up the rod, Israel prevailed. But when he could hold it up no longer, Amalek surged back. This was not due to some magic in the rod, but rather the raised rod coincided with the prayers of Moses.

In this way we have a graphic and biblical example of the sort of divine covering that is promised in Psalm 91.

Word-by-word

HIS TRUTH:	here indicates God's trustworthiness. Many versions say 'his faithfulness'.
SHALL BE YOUR SHIELD:	shields came in different sizes and designs. But really this is a metaphor for the battle of the mind, which is so important in times of war and crisis.
AND BUCKLER:	the shield had to be moved into position to do its work, whereas the buckler was worn as all-round protection. Feathers plus shield plus buckler, a comprehensive belt-and-braces protection against small and large attacks.

Other Versions

- His faithful promises are your armour (LB);
- His constancy is shield and protection (JB);
- His arms fend off all harm (TM).

Prayer

Lord God, please surround me with favour as with a shield today. Lord please strengthen the wall of protection around me, lead me not into temptation, deliver me from evil and all harm. Lord please fill me with your praises and promises and let my words be your words. You are my strength and shield and my defence, O Lord thank you in Jesus' name.

DAY 10:   NO TERROR NONE

V5 You shall not be afraid of the terror of the night

Story

Saudi Desert 4th Feb 1991, the 7th Armoured Brigade. Two chaplains prepare for another denominational service surrounded by guns and ammunition boxes and the paraphernalia of war. Because of religious sensitivities, the two are known as welfare officers. However as evening sets in, 30 men turn up. The service begins with Hymn 42 *Guide us, O heavenly redeemer*. The first chaplain speaks, the wind whips away his voice. The troops shiver, a camouflaged helicopter clatters above.

"Some of you are going to see the things you never dreamed of, and never want to think about again. Perhaps, it will make you question your religion in days to come; but there is a point at which Christians need to be afraid no longer because of their faith and the certainty of resurrection."

Then came Psalm 91, and some unashamed tears on the young faces: quite a few soldiers scribbled verse 5 on their helmet covers "thou shalt not be afraid of the terror of the night." When the small congregation separated into two groups for communion and mass, a pair of renowned American tank busters, warthogs to their admirers flew noisily over in the direction of the Iraq front line, soon there was a crumple of explosions. It was back to business as usual.

Traveller's Tale

One of the most dramatic and inexplicable plagues of Egypt was that of the thick darkness: even during the daytime, some suspension of dust or vapour in the air prevented light from reaching the Egyptians either from the sun or from candles inside houses. Miraculously, although they were equally affected by the darkness outside, the children of Israel were able to use artificial light in their homes. The knowledge that God was with them in the gloom, while the Egyptians were abandoned to their fate, must have been very heartening to the people.

Word-by-word

YOU SHALL NOT BE AFRAID:	means you shall never have reason to — it's a prohibition!
OF THE TERROR:	a wide scope which includes surprise or sudden attack by man, beast or even something demonic.

OF THE NIGHT:	people are naturally apprehensive in the dark as it exposes us to dangers of different kinds that we will have difficulty seeing as they come. So our fears magnify. The Hebrews traditionally divide the day into four periods, evening, midday, midnight, morning. By implication of this psalm each one of these time-slots is covered.

Other Versions

- Now you don't need to be afraid of the dark anymore (LB);
- You need not fear any dangers at night (GN);
- Fear nothing—not wild wolves in the night (TM);
- Thou shalt not need to be afrayed of eny bugges (bugs) by night. Coverdale 1535 Bible (the Bug Bible translates verse 5 as:- beware computer viruses!).

Prayer

Lighten our darkness, Lord we pray; and in your mercy defend us from all perils and dangers of this night; for the love of your only son, our Saviour Jesus Christ.

DAY 11: ARROWS

V5b Nor the arrow that flies by day
[v5b]

Story

After 20 years of ministry in other lands, God led the family of Glen and Peggy Gray to the Ukraine. They were the first Assembly of God missioners to reside in this former communist country. As academic dean, Glen was correlating and organising studies at the Ukrainian Assembly of God Bible School located in the capital Kiev.

The Grays arrived in August 1993, excited about helping to train pastors and leaders for the growing Pentecostal churches. But weeks of discomfort followed, no house, living in one room, no cooker plus visa delays.

They decided on a break. A youth music festival celebrated by the Ukraine churches. A US pastor sensed their discouragement; he prayed for their housing needs. Then before he left, he shook his finger at Glenn and Peggy and said:

"Psalm 91 guys, Psalm 91 is your cover."

"What does that beautiful psalm have to do with our housing?"

About 15 minutes later Peggy, her daughter Charlene and son were sitting in their car (Spirit and Light) outside the hotel where Glen had gone to exchange currencies. Charlene yelled, "Man, that guy has a gun."

As Peggy looked around, she saw a gang surrounding them, other cars and a tourist bus. Peggy screamed for the kids to hit the floor of the car. They did this and Peggy told them to pray that their dad would not walk out into this major robbery. Minutes seemed like hours as they cried to God. Once Peggy peeked out of the car, and saw a man waving his gun wildly. He looked right at Peggy, so she quickly flattened herself down behind the driver's seat again and prayed. The man never came near to their new spirit and light car, an obvious target. Peggy had an overwhelming sense of being covered. In the short time she'd looked up, she'd seen men with guns beating people. Other victims lay bleeding on the ground. Meanwhile, when Glenn tried to leave the hotel, he was almost knocked down by three bandits who were attempting to escape by racing into the hotel lobby. He paused at the door, horrified to see men struggling with armed robbers. In a few minutes he was able to race to the car, where he was relieved to find his family safe. Quickly he drove them away. They returned to the centre where they were staying and George Dawidsk a Ukrainian and US evangelist prayed.

Then without knowing of the previous pastor's prayer, he shook his finger at them and said, "Hey guys! Psalm 91, Psalm 91 is your cover."

Traveller's Tale

In Deuteronomy ch 20, God's laws of warfare are set out. The very first provision is a prohibition of fear, because "The Lord your God is he who goeth with you, to fight for you against your enemies, to save you." [Deut 20:4]. The children of Israel were able to utterly defeat certain peoples and kings who stood in their way: the Traveller particularly remembers the rout of Sihon, King of the Amorites and Og, King of Bashan. Although we are not given figures we can assume a most favourable kill count which can only be explained by God fighting on Israel's side.

Word-by-word

NOR THE ARROW:	as opposed to the more nebulous fears of night attacks, weapons shot in daylight have the advantage of being predictably dangerous and the disadvantage of being more accurately aimed. This can also be applied metaphorically to verbal or psychological attacks.

THAT FLIES BY DAY:	a poetic complement to Night in the line above, so that God promises protection on a 24/7 basis.

Other Versions

- Nor fear the dangers of the day (LB);
- Or sudden attacks during the day (GN);
- Not flying arrows in the day (TM).

Prayer

"If the LORD himself had not been on our side, now may Israel say…" [Ps 124:1] Lord, you have saved our country and members of my own family in conflicts past. Please defend me as well in my hour of need; through Jesus Christ my Lord.

DAY 12: NO FEAR OF STALKING PESTILENCE

V6a Nor the pestilence that walks in the darkness

Story

Lord Cravern lived in London when that sad calamity the plague raged. His house was in that part of town called Cravern Buildings. On the plague reaching epidemic proportions, his lordship, in order to avoid danger, resolved to go to his seat in the country. His coach-and-six were accordingly at the door, his baggage put up, and all things in readiness for the journey. As he was walking through the hall, hat on, cane under his arm, pulling on his gloves, ready to step into his carriage, he overheard his servant saying to another servant

"I suppose, by my Lord's quitting London to avoid the plague, that his God lives in the country and not in the town."

The servant said this in simplicity of heart, as really believing a plurality of Gods. This speech, however struck Lord Cravern very sensibly, and made him pause.

"My God," he thought, "lives everywhere, and can preserve me in town as well as in the country. I will even stay where I am. The ignorance of his servant has just now preached to me a very useful sermon. Lord, pardon my unbelief, and that I distrust of thy providence, which made me think of running from your hand."

He immediately ordered his horses to be taken from the coach, and the baggage to be taken in. He continued to live in London and was remarkable among his sick neighbours by never catching the infection.

Traveller's Tale

First the good news: God has sent quails again, heaps and heaps of them. The people have been up all night netting them and preparing a banquet: now the bad news: [Num 11:33] "While the meat was still between their teeth, before it could be consumed, the anger of the LORD burned against the people, and he struck them with a severe plague". As often, the people were too concerned with their own desires and grumbling against God. So God sent a plague to punish them, perhaps working through their greed (in their haste, could they have failed to cook the birds properly?) But those who spend time in the 'secret place' are less likely to grumble and come under the wrath of God.

Word-by-word

NOR THE PESTILENCE:	in the SYRIAC is rendered blowing wind, blast or hot wind (as from a desert). Includes all infectious diseases and everything that cuts off, removes, carries, snatches away; every sweeping plague that causes devastation.
THAT WALKS IN THE DARKNESS:	mostly poetic, to set up contrast with second half of verse. Could be applied in respect of diseases that come up slowly and imperceptibly like cancer or Alzheimer's. Some versions have 'stalks', like some animal or insect that attacks inside tents when people turn in to sleep.

Other Versions

- Nor dread the plagues of the darkness (LB);
- Or the plagues that strike in the dark (GN);
- Not disease that prowls through the darkness (TM);
- … Stalks in the darkness (ESV, NASB).

Prayer

Father, you have seen the underhand way that my (human and spiritual) enemies steal up on me. I read that you can see as well in the dark as in daylight. So keep me safe at this time.

DAY 13: NO FEAR OF DESTRUCTION

V6b Nor the destruction that lays waste
at noon

London, 1854 the city experiences a major cholera epidemic. A famous Baptist minister Charles Haddon Spurgeon was conducting funerals daily. Long hours of trying to comfort the grieving left the minister feeling frightened, weak and vulnerable. He felt that it was only a matter of time before he succumbed to cholera because of his contact with so many dying people. Spurgeon said,

"I became weary in body and sick at heart. My friends seemed to be falling one by one, and I felt that I was sickening like those around me."

An exhausted Spurgeon was sinking. But that soon changed. Returning from conducting yet another funeral service, a poster in a Shoe-maker's shop window grabbed his attention. The flyer contained sections of Psalm 91, including the heartening words "You will not fear the terror of the night, nor the pestilence that stalks in the darkness, nor the plague that destroys at midday. A thousand may fall at your side, ten thousand at your right hand, but it will not come near you."

The impact of Psalm 91 upon Spurgeon was dramatic; the effect upon his heart immediate.

"I felt secure refreshed, girt with immortality. I went on with my visitation of the dying in a calm peaceful spirit. I felt no fear of evil and suffered no harm. The providence which moved the tradesman to place those verses in his window, I gratefully acknowledge, and in remembrance of its marvellous power, I adore the LORD my God."

Traveller's Tale

"I am immortal until God says I must go." The Traveller was horrified at the invasion of poisonous snakes (almost certainly some form of viper, since adder poison takes time to act on the blood and therefore burns whereas cobra-type poisons act much faster and deaden the nerves so reducing the pain; possibly the saw-scale viper echis carinatus): fortunately God told him to make the famous bronze serpent so that anyone who had the faith to believe it could be saved. Here again, Moses needed to be able to be familiar with and recognise God's voice to be able to get this antidote.

Word-by-word

NOR THE DESTRUCTION:	scourge or sting (like a snakebite).

THAT LAYS WASTE:	more evident than the stalking pestilence of the first part of the verse.
AT NOON:	i.e the hottest part of the day. A poetic counterpoint.

Other Versions

- Nor the disasters of the (early) morning (LB);
- The scourge that wrecks havoc at high noon (JB);
- Nor disaster that erupts at high noon (TM).

Prayer

Lord Almighty, I come to you at the midpoint of the day in your shelter. Deliver me from lightening and tempest; from plague, pestilence and famine; from battle, murder and sudden death that can erupt. Under your providential care we go. In Jesus Christ's name.

DAY 14:   THE BATTLE

V7 A thousand may fall at your side,
and ten thousand at your right hand

Mr Winston Churchill in his description of the
Battle of Malplaquet, quotes from the Diary of
Lieutenant-Colonel J Blackader, an officer of
the Cameronians:

> Among the British battalions which now
> delivered the decisive stroke were the
> Cameronians, and we discern the sombre,
> stately figure of Major Blackader inspiring
> his men and communing with his God, his
> eye fixed upon the Amalekites in another
> Ebenezer of his life. Major Blackader
> records that he never had a more pleasant
> day in his life.

> "The Lord of Hosts went forth at our head
> as captain of our host and the army
> followed with a daring, cheerful boldness,
> for we never doubted we would beat
> them … I was kept in perfect peace; my
> mind stayed, trusting in God. All went
> well with me; and not being in hurry and
> hot action, I had time for plying the
> throne of grace, sometimes by prayer,
> sometimes by praise, as the various turns
> of Providence gave occasion; sometimes
> for the public, sometimes for myself. I did
> not seek any assurance of protection for
> my life; I thought it enough to believe in
> general, to depend with resignation, and
> my hand about his hand."

Mr Churchill adds,

"But if the major had never passed a more pleasant day, it fared otherwise with his Colonel Cranstoun… at the head of his stern regiment. A round shot, about the size of a cricket ball, such as are still picked up in this old battlefield, struck him in the left breast, coming out his back. He fell from his horse before Blackader's eyes without a word. The command devolved upon Blackader, "A thousand shall fall at thy side" he murmured, "and ten thousand at thy right hand; but it shall not once come near to thee". Thus uplifted, in the temper of the ironsides, he led forward his men.

Traveller's Tale

Moses thinks back to the high numbers of casualties at various points: all the firstborn of Egypt; Pharaoh's host; the Midianites and the Amorites and God's command to completely destroy (as being potential causes of temptation) the Hittites, Amorites, Caananites, Perizzites, Hivites and Jebusites [Deut 20:16]. What a privilege to be God's chosen people! How difficult to understand how God deals with those who get in the way. And even among the people of Israel, only two of the adults who crossed the Red Sea went on to cross the Jordan as well.

Word-by-word

A THOUSAND MAY FALL AT YOUR SIDE:	the scene is of a bloody battle in which the dead include both friend and foe.
TEN THOUSAND AT YOUR RIGHT HAND:	a poetic expression for innumerable (like myriad); a right-handed soldier would hold his shield on his left and be more exposed on his right flank. If the person at your right falls, you are even more vulnerable since you can now be attacked by two people on your uncovered side.

Other Versions

- Though a thousand fall at my side, though ten thousand are dying around me (LB);
- A thousand may fall dead beside you, ten thousand all around you, but you will not be harmed (GN);
- Even though others succumb all around, drop like flies right and left, no harm will even graze you (TM).

Prayer

Lord, how are they increased that trouble me! Many are they that rise up against me. Many there be which say, there is no help for him in God. But you O Lord art a shield for me; my glory, and the lifter up of mine head. I cried unto the LORD with my voice, and he heard me out of my holy hill. I laid me down and slept; I awakened; for the LORD sustained me. I WILL NOT BE AFRAID of the ten thousand people, that have set themselves against me round about. Arise, O Lord; save me O my God : for you have smitten all mine enemies upon the cheek bone; you have broken the teeth of the ungodly. Salvation belongs to the LORD; your blessing is upon your people.

DAY 15:   NOT A SINGLE CASUALTY

V7 But it shall not come near you

Story

A bishop braves plague. Horne, in his notes on the Psalms, refers to the plague in Marseilles and the devotion of its bishop. There is a full account of him in *The Percy Anecdotes* from which we cull the following: —

> M. de Belsunce, Bishop of Marseilles, so distinguished himself for his humanity during the plague which raged in that city in 1720, that the Regent of France offered him the richer and more honourable See of Laon, in Picardy; but he refused it, saying he should be unwilling to leave a flock that had been endeared to him by their sufferings. His pious and intrepid labours are commemorated in a picture in the Town Hall of Marseilles, in which he is represented in his episcopal habit, attended by his almoners, giving his benediction to the dying... But perhaps the most touching picture extant of the bishop's humane labours, is to be found in a letter of his own, written to the Bishop of Soissons on September 27, 1720. 'Never,' he says 'was desolation greater, nor was ever anything like this. Here have been many cruel plagues, but none was ever more cruel: to be sick and dead was

almost the same thing. What a melancholy spectacle have we on all sides, we go into the streets full of dead bodies, half rotten through, which we pass to come to a dying body, to excite him to an act of contrition, and to give him absolution.' Notwithstanding exposure to a pestilence so fatal, the devoted bishop escaped uninjured.

Traveller's Tale

The Traveller and the people have detached 12,000 warriors, 1,000 from each tribe to take out a larger number of Midianites [Numbers 31]. After the battle, the sack and capture of enemy chattels, the commanders report back. "Sir, we have counted the soldiers under our command and not one is missing." That is the sort of result to expect when the Living God has taken one side. Interestingly, the soldiers feel they wish to offer an offering of atonement afterwards, perhaps because the heat of battle is rarely completely free of sin: it is also a recognition that God has treated them far better than they deserve.

Word-by-word

BUT IT SHALL NOT COME NEAR:	though in the presence of danger God keeps harm far from us.

YOU:	is emphatic; to you it will not draw near.

Other Versions

- The evil will not touch me (LB);
- But you will not be harmed (GN);
- you yourself will remain unscathed (JB);
- but it shall not approach you (NASB).

Prayer

Father Almighty you love us more than we imagine. You are our Sun and Shield by day, by night you are near our homes and us. No harm will come near us. We worship only you.

DAY 16:   THE REVENGE

*V8 Only with your eyes shall you look
and see the reward of the wicked*

Early the next morning Abraham got up and returned to the place where he had stood before the LORD. He looked down towards Sodom and Gomorrah, towards all the land of the plain and he saw dense smoke rising from the land like smoke from a furnace. So when God destroyed the cities of the plain, he remembered Abraham, and he brought Lot out of the catastrophe that overthrew the cities where Lot had lived. [Genesis 19:27]

Traveller's Tale

"And Israel saw the Egyptian dead upon the seashore." [Exodus 14:30]

The Psalmist is almost certainly thinking of the great day of the miraculous crossing of the Red Sea. The death of the Egyptians upon the sea shore is a glaring symbol of the ultimate doom of evil in its struggle with good. There is something in the very nature of the universe which is on the side of Israel in its struggle with Egypt. There is something in the very nature of the universe which ultimately comes to the aid of goodness in its perennial struggle with evil. There is something in the very nature of the universe which justifies James Russell Lowell in saying:

> Truth forever on the Scaffold
> Wrong forever on the throne.
> Yet that scaffold sways the future,
> And behind the dim unknown
> Stands God within the shadow,
> Keeping watch above his own.
> (Martin Luther King, New York, May 1956)

Now The Traveller seeks God's justice, for vengeance is God's and his alone. From his viewpoint God will let them see the retribution of the wicked for his atrocities and crimes. There is no escaping God's judgement. God is just and Holy!

Word-by-word

ONLY WITH YOUR EYES SHALL YOU LOOK:	"you only need to keep your eyes open to see" (JB)
AND SEE THE REWARD:	some punishments are handed down by men, others seem to be decreed above (though moral relativists may jib at the notion!)
OF THE WICKED:	the wicked are those that wilfully refuse to obey God's moral teachings.

Other Versions

- I will see how the wicked are punished but I will not share in it (LB);
- You will look and see how the wicked are punished (GN);
- You'll stand untouched, watch it all from a distance, watch the wicked turn into corpses (TM).

Prayer

The Light of God surround me the Love of God enfold me the Power of God protect me the Presence of God watch over me wherever I am, God is there.

DAY 17:   THE REFUGE

V9 Because you have made the LORD,
who is my refuge

Story

Psalm 91 as refuge has even featured in film: actress Liv Ullman. playing the part of Dutch woman Kate Ter Horst in the film *A Bridge Too Far*. Her house had become a medical post for the 1st British Airborne Division's costly attempt to seize Arnhem Bridge. In the basement, where up to 200 wounded were being looked after, Psalm 91 was read (in both history and the film).

An ordinary house is hardly a secure refuge in a tank battle. But if God protects the house, it can be. Similarly if the bravery of Kate ter Horst earned her the nickname 'the Angel of Arnhem', think how much more help a real angel would be in a time of crisis.

Lieutenant Cleminson, 3rd Parachute Battalion, was in the house with a wound in his arm. He said that every morning she would come around reading Psalm 91 and encourage people. He said that she was a fantastic women who kept up everyone's courage.

Traveller's Tale

The Traveller thinks again of his interviews with Pharaoh (while the real intention was to quit Egypt completely, negotiations centred around offering worship to YHWH in the wilderness). In a real sense, the name and prestige of the God of Abraham, Isaac and Jacob was at stake in the showdown with Pharaoh. So this was also a way of saying that God was their refuge.

'God is our refuge and strength, an ever-present help in trouble.'

Word-by-word

BECAUSE YOU HAVE MADE:	YOU is emphatic. This is a choice.
THE LORD:	YHWH compare v. 2a.
WHO IS MY REFUGE:	note the possessive 'my'. As we saw above, refuge has a legal as well as a physical dimension. A place of trust, a place for protection and a place to confide intimately together.

Other Versions

- For Jehovah is my refuge (LB);
- You had made the Lord your defender (GN);
- For you have made the LORD, my refuge (NASB);
- You who say "Yahweh my refuge!" (JB).

Prayer

How precious is your steadfast love, O God! The children of men take refuge in the shadow of your wings. They feast on the abundance of your house, and you give them drink from the river of your delights. For with you is the fountain of life; in your light do we see light. [Psalm 36:7-9]

DAY 18:   HOME

V9 Even the Most High your habitation

Story

In the early days of aviation there was a pioneer flyer named Handley Page. Page often flew to India. During one of his flights he landed in a meadow. After resting a while, Page returned to his plane and took off. He had been in the air only a short time when he heard a gnawing sound behind him. He realized instantly what had happened. While on the ground, a rat had boarded his plane.

Page fearfully listened as the rat gnawed away on some important wires right behind his head. He feared the rat would disable his craft and send it plummeting to the earth. In a panic, Page suddenly recalled that rats can only live at low altitudes. Immediately he raised the plane's nose to the sun and flew as high as he and his craft could withstand. The air was so thin he could hardly breathe. He stayed at that altitude for the duration of his flight. When he landed, he looked behind him and found the rat. It was dead, suffocated by the altitude. So here we see it is important for us to remember to fly high and stay close to God. If we stay with the process he has ordained and fly as high as we can, he'll take care of the rest. So keep your eyes on him, and he'll deal with the rats!

Traveller's Tale

'Where is our home?' the Traveller asks himself. It's no longer Egypt where we were born, nor the promised land which we have not yet conquered. Our nomadic tents pitched in the desert are the best we can do, humanly speaking. But spiritually, we wanderers are forced to recognise our reliance on God, who is the only ultimate source of protection. The God he and his people are counting on is omnipotent, omniscient, omnipresent and will be with them on the way.

Word-by-word

EVEN THE MOST HIGH:	Elyon, as in verse 1 where the secret place is 'of Elyon'.
YOUR HABITATION:	home is a natural place to be, does not require effort once the choice of its location is made. Some versions translate as 'fortress'.

Other Versions

- I choose the God above all other gods to shelter me (LB);

- the Most High your protector (GN);
- the High God your very own home (TM);
- the Most High, who is my refuge (ESV);
- and make Elyon your fortress (JB).

Prayer

Lord, let not my heart be troubled for in your Father's house are many rooms; if it were not so, you would have told me. Thank you, Lord, that you have gone to prepare a place for me and that you will come again to take me to yourself so that where you are, I will be also.

DAY 19:   NO EVIL WILL STRIKE YOU

V10 No evil will befall you

Story

Yugoslavia 1999, Aleksandra the official reader of the Svelto evangelistic team just finished a meeting in Grdelica. "The inhabitants have been experiencing terrible fear and shock. Although they came unannounced, the little house filled soon with children and their parents. At the end they had to go outside and have their service in the back yard. Sunchica played the guitar, Aleksandra read the Psalms, Zoran spoke on the end times, and Biljana, our one month old convert, helped out with the singing. But, before leaving, the believers insisted "In the Shadow of His Wings" to be sung again. It has become the most demanded song in the churches across Yugoslavia. So, the group began singing the lyrics based on Psalm 91. As they were singing the chorus they could hear the roar of planes above their heads. It became louder and louder. The non-believing neighbours, who stood by the fence, left the yard and ran to their basements for safety. The believers remained and moved closer together while continuing to sing the words of the

Psalm. The planes were nearer. They sang louder. Until the roar of the planes out voiced them. Then a detonation shook the ground. A sudden pause in singing. Are we all OK? Realizing that the explosion must have occurred elsewhere, somewhere over the hills, they gathered courage and continued singing. The second and the third detonation didn't disrupt the song. Now they had the confirmation that they were under His wings, and that no missile flying at daytime nor any destruction at noonday would come near them.

Traveller's Tale

Infanticide: one of the worst crimes that anyone can commit. But it was the command of Pharaoh, to kill all the Hebrew male children. Every time he hears his own name, The Traveller is reminded of how close he came to sharing such a fate. It was an evil indeed, and the infant Moses was threatened by it.

Nevertheless, what had seemed a deprivation at the time – separation from family – turned into an opportunity to learn skills necessary for saving the whole people. So not everything that starts with man's evil motives ends up as calamity. God can and does rescue.

Word-by-word

NO EVIL:	the meaning here is very wide including all perils, ills and misfortunes. Could also mean a wound inflicted on a person. A general as 'deliver us from evil'.
WILL BEFALL YOU:	the imperfect tense has the force of a promise: 'No disaster can overtake you' (JB)

Other Versions

- How then can evil overtake me (LB);
- And so no disaster will strike you (GN);
- Evil can't get close to you (TM);
- No evil shall be allowed to befall you (ESV).

Prayer

The Lord shall preserve me from all evil; He shall preserve my soul. The Lord shall preserve my going out and my coming in. From this time forth, and even for evermore. [Psalm 121:7-8]

DAY 20: NO PLAGUE NEAR YOU

V10b Nor shall any plague come near your dwelling

Story

Although Defoe's history of the plague is a work of fiction, its statements are generally factual and therefore we extract the following:–

"The misery of the poor I had many occasions to be an eyewitness of, and sometimes also of the charitable assistance that some pious people daily gave to such, sending them relief and supplies both of food, physic, and other help as they found they wanted... Some pious ladies were transported with zeal in so good a work, and so confident in the protection of Providence in discharge of the great duty of charity, that they went about in person distributing alms to the poor, and even visiting poor families, though sick and infected, in their very houses, appointing nurses to attend those that wanted attending, and ordering apothecaries and surgeons... giving their blessing to the poor in substantial relief to them, as well as hearty prayers for them. I will not undertake to say, as some do, that none of those charitable people were suffered to fall under the calamity itself; but this I may say, that I never knew anyone of them that came to any ill, which I mention for the encouragement of others in case of the like distress, and, doubtless, if they that give to the poor lend to the LORD, and he will repay them, those that hazard their lives to give to the poor, and to comfort and assist the poor in such misery as this, may hope to be protected in the work."

"England may congratulate herself on having cherished in her bosom a clergyman who in an equally earnest manner discharged his pastoral care, and watched over the simple flock committed to his charge, at no less risk of life, and with no less fervour of piety and benevolence. [Daniel Defoe's *Journal of the Plague in London*]

Traveller's Tale

"Miriam's skin was suddenly covered with a dreaded disease" [Numbers 12:10]. She had been criticising Moses for marrying a foreign woman. So despite having seen God's power at work all through the Exodus, Miriam was punished, though in the end God allowed her to be healed [vs 15].

The promise contained in this psalm is conditional on staying close to God. There is no assurance of holding on to the benefits apart from staying close to God and regularly asking forgiveness for any wrong.

Word-by-word

NOR SHALL ANY PLAGUE:	any dangerous epidemic, not just bubonic plague. There is a connotation of divine judgement in the word.
COME NEAR YOUR DWELLING:	the word for dwelling means tent, reflecting the nomadic way of life.

Other Versions

- Or any plague come near (LB);
- no violence will come near your home (GN);
- harm can't get through the door (TM);
- nor will any plague come near your tent (NASB).

Prayer

> God's shield to protect me,
> God's legion to save me
> from snares of the demons
> from evil enticements
> from plagues near me
>
> from failings of nature
> from one man or many
> that seek to destroy me
> near or afar.
>
> [St Patrick's Breastplate p 22]

DAY 21: THE GUARDIANS

V11 For He shall give His angels charge over you

Story

On 23 August 1914, a British Army unit advanced to Mons in Belgium. To their astonishment they walked straight into a German division who promptly attacked with superior numbers and weapons. But the Germans faced a tremendous counterattack not from the British but from a band of angels who threw a protective curtain around the British while phantom bowman repelled the Germans. This episode was known as *The Angel of Mons.* The historian A.J.P Taylor was convinced that the event took place, he said that the supernatural intervention was observed more-or-less reliably by the British soldiers.

The Bible teaches that there are angels and tells us that their role is to minister to God's people. Tradition holds that there were three archangels Michael, Gabriel and Lucifer until the last was cast out of heaven. So it is less surprising he quotes this verse at Jesus misrepresenting the meaning of the sentence.

St Thomas Aquinas accepted from Maimonides the view that a greater measure of the gifts of freewill and reason had been bestowed on angels than on mankind. He also believed prophetic revelation was accomplished by the agency of angels.

Traveller's Tale

"I will send my angel before you to protect you as you travel and to bring you to the place I have prepared. Pay attention to him and obey him" [Ex 23:20f]. The Traveller is guaranteed an escort from God of angelic bodyguards. Angels also seem to be empowered to minister healing {Ex 23:25f}. The Hebrews had the pillar of cloud, but we need to seek God's guidance in the secret place: and keep our eyes open for divine hints.

Word-by-word

HE SHALL GIVE HIS ANGELS:	note the plural. They are spiritual agents of God's providential cover over us all.

CHARGE OVER YOU:	a strict chain of command is implied. YOU means his people. He does not assign a solitary angel to each saint, but commissions whole armies of heaven. This passage does not exclude a guardian angel, but shows that angels can have varied roles.

Other Versions

- God will put his angels in charge of you to protect you wherever you go (GN);
- He ordered his angels to guard you wherever you go (TM);
- For he will command his angels concerning you to guard you in all your ways (NRSV).

Prayer

O Eternal God, who has ordained and constituted the services of angels and men in a wonderful order, mercifully grant that as your holy angels always do you service in him, so by your appointment may succour and defend us on earth through Jesus Christ, our Lord.

DAY 22: KEPT IN ALL YOUR WAYS

V11b To keep you in all your ways

Story

A story from Lima, Peru by David Gates who was working with a church. He had been to collect valuable computer equipment in the port but unfortunately his car needed a push start. What is worse, on the way back his engine cut out in a 'bad' street. He needed a push, preferably from several people.

Only it was evening and soon a couple of unsavoury-looking characters were observing him. They picked up rocks and began to threaten. With a prayer to God, Gates decided to stand his ground, for the sake of the equipment; suddenly out of nowhere a Spanish-looking gentleman appeared with a memorable and flawless face. He offers to push the car, but it looked doubtful as it was on gravel and facing uphill.

But he insisted and Gates got in his car. Under the noses of the baddies, he gave a great heave and the car engine started. Gates made his escape.

The Bible says that "Some of you have entertained angels unawares" [Heb. 13:2].

Sometimes it is hard to distinguish between a human sent by God and an angel: but certainly the sudden appearance, the beauty, and the extraordinary strength made it feel like the second.

Traveller's Tale

The Traveller's thoughts turn to Balaam and the slightly comical story of how his donkey was more perceptive than he. "I have come here to oppose you, because your path is a reckless one before me" [Numbers 22:32], spoke the angel who was ready to kill Balaam if necessary. Meeting an angry angel is no picnic.

Word-by-word

TO KEEP YOU:	to hedge about, to attend to, to preserve, save, defend and preserve
IN ALL YOUR WAYS:	means 'wherever you go' but also with a hint of 'keep you on track' (compare 'charge' in first half).

Other Versions

- To protect you wherever you go (LB, GN);
- Defend and preserve in all your ways (of obedience and service) (AMP).

Prayer

Father Almighty God of all angels – send your watchful angels. But, lo, a place has been prepared for me, whom watchful angels keep; yes, he himself becomes my guard, he smooths my bed and gives me sleep.

I bind unto myself today – the power of God to hold and lead, his eye to watch, his might to stay, his ear to hearken to my need, the wisdom of my God to teach, his hand to guide, his shield to ward, the word of God to give me speech, his heavenly host to be my guard.

DAY 23:   BORNE UP

V12 They shall bear you up in their hands lest you dash your foot against a stone.

Story

Today we turn our thinking to the famous time when Satan quoted this psalm to Jesus, tempting him to launch down from the pinnacle of the temple: I would suggest that we can sum up all three temptations in the theory that they were all forms of 'power solution' that avoided the cross.

I am sure that Jesus indeed had, or could summon from his Father, the power to execute each and any of the three, just as he could have avoided the cross. But his calling was on a higher plane than mere human success. Therefore, the fact that this psalm offers cast-iron guarantees of safety does not imply that avoiding risk or injury is always the best choice for Christians. In fact some of the greatest acts of valour both spiritually and in the military are taken by people plunging into danger when they could have stayed safe.

There is a pagan Latin proverb that 'fortune favours the brave' and the Psalmist might concur, while substituting his infinite God for 'fortune'. But the psalm's teaching that there is a safe place to escape to does not mean that a believer who voluntarily risks his life for love of his neighbour will not pay the price.

Traveller's Tale

"Take the rod ... speak to the rock." But sadly the Traveller understood this as speak to the people (in fairly bad tempered tone) and strike the rock; indeed he struck it *twice* [Numbers 20]. For this failure of faith, he was not to lead the people into Canaan; but nevertheless he was not removed from leadership, so we can see it as a stumble but not a fall. In terms of our verse, the angels caught him.

In a previous incident of water from a rock [Ex 17], God said "I will stand on the rock" which may well mean his angel was there (Paul later suggested that the rock was Christ). So failure to see the risen Christ (or his Angel) can lead to missing part of one's call.

Word-by-word

THEY SHALL BEAR YOU UP IN THEIR HANDS:	this is an amplification of their charge over us. Angels not only lead but are ready to catch you if you stumble.

LEST YOU DASH YOUR FOOT AGAINST A STONE:	notice stones are not taken out of your way but you are kept from injury.

Other Versions

- They will steady you with their hands to keep you from stumbling against the rocks on the trail (LB);
- They will hold you up with their hands, to keep you from hurting your feet on the stones (GN);
- If you stumble, they'll catch you; their job is to keep you from falling (TM).

Prayer

'Let him that thinks he stands take heed lest he fall:' Father send your angels so they may prepare the way ahead, or if I begin to go wrong, rescue me from a terminal error.

DAY 24:   THE ATTACK

V13 You shall tread upon the lion and the cobra

Story

Mary Slessor, the Calabrar Missionary under Psalm 91, was never once stung by countless poisonous snakes that abounded in the Calabrar, nor was she ever attacked by savage animals although often her errands of mercy led her through dense jungle teeming with leopards. Even at night she heard their blood curdling cries near her but passed unharmed, praying, "O God of Daniel shut their mouths."

Traveller's Tale

A snake trick! God had prepared the Traveller with a miracle of a staff that turned into a snake [Exod 7]. And when Pharaoh's magicians did likewise, then Aaron's snake ate the other ones! In a metaphorical sense, Pharaoh was both a lion and a cobra: the lion part was the sheer violence of forced labour. The cobra part was the subtle nastiness: Pharaoh thought they were asking for a holiday so he increased their workload instead.

Word-by-word

YOU SHALL TREAD UPON:	in addition to angelic help, you will have the power to overcome and destroy fierce enemies who are full of venom and fury.
THE LION:	was a real danger in those days in Palestine. David fought and killed lions. A metaphor for open violence.
AND THE COBRA:	or asp: probably the deadly Egyptian Cobra. In a metaphoric sense, a more hidden but equally dangerous attacker.

Other Versions

- You can safely meet a lion or step on a poisonous snake (LB);
- You'll walk unharmed among lions and snakes (TM);
- You will overpower the strongest lions and the most deadly snakes (CEV).

Protection

May God shield me,
May God fill me,

May God keep me,
May God watch me,
May God bring me
To the land of peace,
To the country of the King,
To the place of eternity.

Prayer

Father, in line with your will I go into the fight: help me be alert and attack, bind, hit my enemy no matter how fierce or ruthless. Let me stamp down on my enemy in victory. I pray this in the name of Jesus Christ, to whom be all the glory.

DAY 25:   THE TRAMPLING

V13b The young lion and the serpent
you shall trample under foot

Story

Trampling is slightly more aggressive than treading; also attack is often the best form of defence. An interesting example of this was the pre-emptive strike by the Israeli Air Force against the Egyptians in 1967. It was apparently inspired by Moshe Dayan's reading of the famous story of David and Goliath. The lesson of that story is that David won the battle by changing the rules in his own favour. Goliath imagined there was a 'rule' for starting such fights, and in fact lost before he thought the battle had started.

As David said to Saul "when [the lion] arose against me, I caught him by his beard, and smote him and slew him." It was less dangerous to take a firm initiative than to wait in hope of killing a charging beast. So this psalm can give us the confidence to lessen risk by attacking first (though this is not a blanket moral justification of first strike!).

Traveller's Tale

The negotiations with Pharaoh got tougher each time: the king started offering compromises, why don't you sacrifice to God here in Egypt? Then he suggests (taking the name of the LORD in vain) that by insisting on taking women and children rather than men only, Moses is bent on rebellion.

Pharaoh was not completely wrong in his intuition that there was more to Moses' plan than a week's retreat; but Moses 'trampled' on him by refusing any compromises.

Word-by-word

THE YOUNG LION:	mostly a poetic repetition; young lions have to be more aggressive to find their place in the sun.
AND THE SERPENT:	amplifies the naturalistic 'cobra' with all the connotations of malice in the word 'serpent'. Also means dragon and sea monster.
YOU WILL TRAMPLE UNDER FOOT:	trample again is stronger than tread, for poetic effect.

Other Versions

- Kick young lions and serpents from the path (TM);

- You will crush fierce lions and serpents under your feet (NLT)!

Prayer

Father, thank you! You have given us the authority to trample on snakes and scorpions and to overcome all the power of the enemy. Nothing will harm us.

DAY 26: YOU WILL BE DELIVERED

V14 Because he has set his love upon me,
therefore I will deliver him

Story

Shelter Now aid workers Heather Mercer and Diana Curry lay in the hands of the Taliban. If found guilty of trying to spread the Gospel of Christ in Afghanistan they would be put to death. In this period Diana, believed Heather would benefit from reflecting on Psalm 91. Heather said, "The Psalm gave me confidence. I read it out loud and v14 specifically touched my heart. That is, God would save us out of prison simply because we loved him." In fact, 102 days later they were released.

Traveller's Tale

One thing the Traveller can never forget: God loved us long before we loved him. He spelled this out in Deuteronomy 7:8. God chose the Hebrews because he loved them and had made promises to their fathers, not for any quality he found in them. And, in the same chapter, we see that he expected the chosen people to respond in love by being set apart or holy from other peoples. They were to make no treaty with them nor intermarry nor worship any of their idols (nor even rework the gold and silver on the same idols). Holiness is our response to God's love.

Word-by-word

BECAUSE HE HAS:	human input is important
SET HIS LOVE ON ME:	Hebrew verb signifying to desire, to love or to find delight in any object. Can also mean cling to. Love is a conscious choice here rather than a feeling.
THEREFORE I WILL DELIVER HIM:	the Psalmist makes God utter a strong direct promise in the first person. Deliverance implies that we cannot save ourselves.

Other Versions

- God says, "I will save those who love me and will protect those who acknowledge me as Lord" (GN);
- "If you'll hold on to me for dear life," says God, "I'll get you out of any trouble. I'll give you the best of care if you'll only get to know and trust me" (TM);
- "Because he has loved Me, therefore I will deliver him; I will set him securely on high, because he has known My name" (NASB).

Prayer

Father, God of love, who cares for me and wants the best more than I can imagine, how priceless is your unfailing love. Both high and low among men find refuge in the shadow of your wings. You are ever ready to swoop down and deliver.

> My mouth praises thee with joyful lips, when I think of thee upon my bed, and meditate on thee in the watches of the night; for thou hast been my help, and in the shadow of thy wings I sing for joy. My soul clings to thee; thy right hand upholds me. [Psalm 63:5-8]

DAY 27:   HIGH TOWER

V14b I will set him high, because
he has known my name

Story

A couple of eaglets fall from their lofty nest and
are raised by turkeys. They grow up thinking
they belong to the crowd, but neither one can
ever get excited over the turkey kind of things.
One of the eaglets is half-heartedly engaged in
a hunt for acorns.

He was dragging behind the crowd and he
stopped under a tree. His head was down, his
wings were dropped and he was saying, "O
Lord, another day."

There was an owl sitting up in the tree. He
looked down from his limb and saw that
bedraggled looking eaglet – defeated and dis-
couraged. The owl asked,

"Who-o-o are you? And what's wrong?"

The eaglet answered, "I'm a turkey that's
failing. I have tried so hard, but I can't make it. I
don't even want to finish another day."

The owl said, "Your problem is you don't
know who-o-o-o you are. You're an eagle.
Eagles are meant to be up there in the sky. You
will never be happy down there on the ground
in the dark woods."

I know a man who lived in a fairly rough area and who believed in God sincerely. Through a set of circumstances he was moved to a classy area in London. As he looked out of his window four floors above London he realised the truth of this fable.

Knowing God's name and character is the best antidote to focusing on self, idols or vain imaginations.

Traveller's Tale

"Moses was a humble man, more humble than any man on earth" [Numbers 12:2]. This is a huge paradox: an epoch-making leader, the one with whom God spoke face-to-face, the one to whom was entrusted the Torah, how come he was so humble?

The revelations at Horeb, where he first learned the name I AM, and subsequently learned of God's character through the law must have revealed to him how far he fell short of God's holiness. And that inward mourning for his own and his people's sinfulness was the first step in God's work of grace in his heart.

Word-by-word

I WILL SET HIM HIGH:	means beyond reach of danger, a safe place out of harm's way.

BECAUSE HE HAS KNOWN MY NAME:	names in the Bible do not just denote someone, but indicate character.

Other Versions

- I will make him great because he trusts in my name (LB);
- And will protect those who acknowledge me as Lord (GN);
- I will set him securely on high, because he has known My name (NASB).

Prayer

Father at the name of Jesus every knee shall bow. If we ask anything in your name you will do it. Believing you! Relying on you! O Jesus, I have promised to serve you to the end; be you ever near me, my master and my friend; I shall not fear the battle if you are by my side, nor wander from the pathway if you will be my guide. (Song by Basil Harwood).

DAY 28:   CRY OUT

V15 He shall call upon me, and
I will answer him

Story

When the British forces were driven back to
Dunkirk, France, the 16th Army had nowhere
else to go except into the sea. Anguished
prayers were said in churches and homes
throughout the United Kingdom. Churchill
thought that only 30,000 would survive and
over 350,000 would be lost. Then two extraordinary things happened: inexplicably, Hitler
ordered his armoured divisions which were
approaching Dunkirk to stop and pull back;
and the heavy seas in the Channel abated,
allowing the navy and a flotilla of little ships to
take off nearly 400,000 British, French and
Belgian troops. "Truly a direct answer to
prayer said the then Archbishop of Canter-
bury. 'A miraculous deliverance!' commented
Churchill.

> Therefore, children, right from the cradle
> one should begin to pray for the princes,
> for their brethren and companions. For
> here you hear the command and the
> promise: 'ask, and it will be given you;
> seek and you will find; knock and the
> door will be opened to you' [Matthew

7:7]. You have been commanded to pray and promised that what you pray for will be given you, as in Psalm 50:15 'Call upon me in the day of trouble and I will deliver you, and you shall glorify me,' and in Psalm 91:5, 'When he calls to me, I will answer him.'

So go on and say : "Now I know that my prayer is not to be despised; for if I despise it, I despise the command and the promise of God." But God does not despise prayer, but rather he has commanded it and promised that he will hear it. Why then should I despise it? But we live like the wild beasts when we do not pray. [Martin Luther]

Traveller's Tale

God will honour any heart's sincere call for help; but knowing God's character, and spending time in the secret place with him, allows for a more confident request.

The Traveller has certainly done his share of intercession for his people. He has prayed for guidance and deliverance and forgiveness from their errors. He has prayed to stop the various plagues of Egypt and all the judgments of the desert wanderings.

So intimate with God did Moses become after 40 days on the Mount Sinai that his face began to shine, and for a time he needed to wear a veil so as not to dazzle his compatriots! [Ex 34:29]

Word-by-word

HE SHALL CALL ME:	the same one whom God has lifted up because he knows God. The request for help may be on his own behalf or for others.
AND I WILL ANSWER HIM:	sometimes God takes the initiative in acts of deliverance: more often he wants us to ask him first. God always answers, though sometimes the content is unexpected.

Other Versions

- Call me and I'll answer (TM);
- When they call to me, I will answer them (NRSV);
- Since he clings to me, I rescue him (JB).

Prayer

May the LORD hear us in the day of trouble; the name of the God of Jacob defend us; send us help from his sanctuary and strengthen us out of Zion; remember all your offerings and accept our burnt sacrifice; grant us your heart's desire and fulfil all our mind. [Psalm 20.1-4]

DAY 29:   GOD WITH YOU

V15b I will be with him in trouble. I will deliver him and honour him

Story

Enquirer: "Rabbi to what can this utterance be compared? Rabbi: "To a pregnant woman who had a quarrel with her mother. Her mother went upstairs and when the daughter was giving birth, she was crying out downstairs and her mother upstairs was listening to her voice and she was crying out also, echoing her daughter. Her neighbour woman was saying to her. "What's going on? Are you giving birth along with her?" She said, "My daughter is having trouble giving birth. Even though she made me angry, I cannot bear her crying out, so I am crying out along with her." This points to the whole covenant of a suffering God along with humanity. This can only be understood in the covenant community, which involves God in the destiny of his fellow members.

Walking down the street, Corrie Ten Boom (in *The Hiding Place*) felt a sudden darkness. She didn't feel God's presence. Later in his word, God assured her that he was so close she was sensing his shadow.

Traveller's Tale

An incident in the life of our Traveller illustrates the 3-step process envisaged here.

Grumbling is part of a leader's lot, but it came to a head in Numbers 12 when his natural brother and sister began to join in. But God picked up the rumblings even before Moses, and took the initiative to stage a showdown: he solved the issue by pointing out how superior Moses was to an ordinary prophet and underlined this by insisting that Miriam did not get away too lightly. Moses did not have to lift a finger or make a plea, but God undertook for his honour.

Word-by-word

I WILL BE WITH HIM IN TROUBLE:	the most graphic example in the Bible is in the Book of Daniel, where three Jews are thrown into the furnace and onlookers see a fourth silhouette with them. Literally, as soon as trouble comes.
I WILL DELIVER HIM:	the second of three steps: presence – deliverance – follow up. John 16:33 'In the world you will have trouble and sorrow…'

AND HONOUR HIM:	'...but rejoice, I have conquered the world.' God not only saves, but the process of suffering with God actually increases any man's spiritual stature.

Other Versions

- I will be with him in trouble and rescue him and honour him (LB);
- When they are in trouble I will be with them. I will rescue them and honour them (GN);
- ... Be at your side in bad times; I'll rescue you, then throw you a party (TM);
- I will be with him in trouble; I will rescue him and honour him (RSV/ NASB).

Prayer

Lord, upon our blindness,
your pure radiance pour;
for your loving kindness
make us love you more;
and when clouds are drifting
dark across our sky,
then, the veil uplifting,
Father, be you near,
    [From a Song by William How, adapted]

DAY 30:   A FULL LIFE AND COMPLETE SALVATION

V16 With long life, I will satisfy him and show him My salvation

Story

In Jerusalem around 4BC, there was a man, Simeon by name, a good man, a man who lived in prayerful expectancy of help for Israel. And the Holy Spirit was on him. The Holy Spirit had shown him that he would see the Messiah of God before he died. Led by the Spirit, he entered the temple. As the parents of the child Jesus brought him in to carry out the rituals of the Law, Simeon took the baby into his arms and blessed God:

"God, you can now release your servant; release me in peace as you promised. With my own eyes I've seen your salvation; it's now out in the open for everyone to see: a God-revealing light to the non-Jewish nations, and of glory for your people Israel."

Traveller's Tale

From the top of Mount Nebo on the 'wrong' side of the Jordan River the Traveller looks over the Promised Land, as YHWH himself points out to him its length and breadth. He hears God's promise to Abraham, Isaac and Jacob reiterated.

"Moses was a hundred and twenty years old when he died; he was as strong as ever and his eyesight was still good" [Deut 34:7].

Moses' obituary [Deut 34:12]: "No other prophet has been able to do the great and terrifying things that Moses did in the sight of all Israel." Knowing God more intimately than any other, Moses could move serenely across the metaphorical Jordan that separates the present from everlasting life. The shadow of the Almighty was helping him go through the valley of the shadow of death.

Word-by-word

WITH LONG LIFE I WILL SATISFY HIM:	satisfaction is almost more important than length of days. And perhaps the greatest source of satisfaction is the faith that our hope is not for this life only.

AND SHOW HIM MY SALVATION:	'grant him to see my salvation' (JB). Salvation is a gift of God, and not something earned by merit. It is not just deliverance from the present crisis but a new status before God. Although salvation is plainly written into scripture, no one can come to Jesus except the Father draw him. Salvation is always God's initiative.

Other Versions

- I will satisfy him with a full life and give him my salvation (LB).
- I will reward them with long life; I will save them. rescue you, then throw you a party (GN);
- I'll give you a long life, give you a long drink of salvation (TM)!
- "With a long life I will satisfy him and let him see My salvation"(NASB).

Prayer

Make this my Lord's accepted hour; come, O my soul's physician to me! Display your justifying power, and show me your salvation now. Help me to live joyfully and die joyfully. Fill me with length of days and revel in your amazing grace and SALVATION [based on C. Wesley hymn]

QUESTIONS AND

DISCUSSION POINTS

This Psalm declares great promises from God and outlines the simple condition for claiming them. What is the key condition on which all the promises of God depend on?

1. To whom are the promises of verses 3 and 8 addressed?

2. What does it mean to dwell and to rest?

3. Why is their need of his protection?

4. What indicates that the dangers are very real and not just imaginary?

5. How can God be your refuge and dwelling place?

6. What new promises are made in verses 10-13?

7. Who is the first speaker and who is the last speaker in this Psalm?

8. The promises of verses 14-16 what areas of human need do they cover?

9. Acrostic: try to name 8 promises starting with each letter of SHADOWER

TERRORISM: SEEKING A CHRISTIAN ANALYSIS

"The purpose of terrorism is to produce terror," said Vladmir Lenin, the Russian Communist Leader responsible for the red terror of 1917-21. The basic mechanism of terror was captured in an ancient Chinese proverb: kill one, frighten ten thousand.

David's psalm is about fear and violence in general rather than specifically about terrorism. But terrorism has a particular resonance because it is quite deliberate, almost methodical, in thinking through ways and means of maximising the fearful payoff of its actions. In fact it is quite difficult to agree a definition of terrorism. Here is an official American attempt: [US code, sectn 2656f(d)]

> The term terrorism means premeditated, politically motivated violence perpetuated against non combatant targets by subnational groups or clandestine agents, usually intended to influence an audience.

Here is another taken from Thomas Perry Thornton :

> A symbolic act designed to influence
> political behaviour by extranormal means,
> entailing the use or threat of violence.

These two are rather wide, which can be politically useful in order to label groups as 'terrorist' but I prefer to propose my own rather tighter ha'penny worth:

> Terrorism is a methodology for self-appointed conspirators to champion a stateless or repressed cause: it combines intimidation of the victim constituency with spectacular token outrages against the oppressor.

1) A methodology: some political causes are worthier than others and there are different strategies for furthering a given cause. It is useful to separate cause from method, because a right cause can be pursued by unjust means, just as it is by no means rare to see a bad cause triumph at the ballot box through persuasion fair and foul. Political causes stretch from *résistance* movements (after a military annexation) through separatists seeking autonomy for a new state. Failed revolutionaries, religious fanatics, local war lords – all have causes which could be furthered by terrorist tactics. The scope of causes is so wide that no reader is likely to be immune from terrorist threat at some point!

2) Self-appointed conspirators: the sign that terrorists are usually self-appointed is that often more than one group springs up to uphold a given cause. The self-appointment may be a solemn oath or it may arise from a spontaneous act of anger. Sometimes self-appointment is a convenient myth, when in fact the secret services of one government are fomenting troubles: our definition would suggest this something different from (worse than) pure terrorism. Such covert acts are neither stateless nor self-appointed and their outrages of such sponsored terrorists are all the worse for enjoying greater resources. But the convenient diplomatic deniability in fact relies on the assumption that the group is self-appointed and stateless.

3) Champion a stateless or repressed cause: the championing is a claim to heroism while the repression justifies the means and the venom of terrorist attacks. This phrase is supposed to exclude parties to an international or civil war which control troops and territory and are surely not terrorists even if their actions are savage or they sponsor terrorism as in (2) above. Championing also implies a claim to legitimacy and leadership over against any 'quisling' administration who works with the 'oppressors'.

4) Intimidation of a victim constituency: a key point of my definition is that terrorism presupposes at least *three groups:* the conspirators, an oppressor (normally a government) and a target 'constituency' which is caught between oppression by the official government and intimidation by the terrorists. A dictatorial régime typically may play the role of oppressor but not that of conspirator. The conspirators expect money, safe houses and the respect due to the effective police of the community, while collaborators, institutions and even moderates are discredited. The intimidation extends to press ganging for recruits and compromising the livelihood of the very people they seek to represent. For Christians believers caught in the crossfire of intimidation and repression, the miraculous deliverance from malicious snares and curses promised in the Psalm is particularly relevant.

5) *Spectacular token outrages*: 'token' is a crucial part of the distinction between terrorism and the more extensive and direct violence of open warfare. In particular even outrages contrary to the rules of war perpetrated by troops of rogue states or guerrilla units are clearly a step beyond terrorism, if they are preludes to devastation that is no longer 'token'.

From first principles, the Christian church must recognise that there are believers on both sides of any conflict, and therefore must be reluctant to take sides. But at first sight, from this definition of terrorism, I can see three moral problems with terrorism: (1) "irresponsibility" in the sense that the terrorists are imposing a violent bid for political leadership on a repressed constituency that has no way of calling them to account; (2) the methods of intimidation are evil in themselves and may do more actual mischief over the long term than the spectaculars. Finally the discrediting of the authorities leads to a breakdown of law and order, and over time to impoverishment.

Real world examples and complications

In real-world situations, there can be more than one oppressor, more than one constituency and competing terrorist organisations – British readers need only think of Ulster! Civil wars are different from terrorism but have a natural link with it: typically a successful terrorist campaign can lead to open rebellion. Or the losing side may resort to a terrorist endgame.

A typical instance of true double-persecution keep-the-cause-alive terrorism in 2005 would be in Sri Lanka where the Tamil population and their political leadership are caught between repression and suspicion from the authorities and the obedience, refuge, service, money expected by the terrorists. Such people are in a thoroughly unpleasant no-win situation while their economic well-being is also undermined.

Outrages will always cause innocent victims to suffer, but not every one is a terrorist act: often wars are started by some symbolic outrage which in effect 'crosses the Rubicon'. Diplomacy often keeps the lead-up to war wrapped in mystery. Famously, for instance, it is not clear how to consider the assassination of Archduke Franz Ferdinand in Sarajevo: was this an act of hothead Serb terrorism, or was it – as the Austrians understood it – a deliberate machination by Belgrade with a view to fomenting war?

Zimbabwe in the 1970s was an example of a terrorist methodology playing out over the long term for the benefit of the perpetrators. During the time of the white Unilateral Declaration of Independence (an attempt by colonists to change the terms of decolonisation as imposed by London), left-leaning guerrilla groups including ZANU, already existing prior to UDI, stepped up their terrorist acts. These were never going to lead to military victory: but they did have the effect of encouraging as many white Rhodesians as could hang on to UK passports to keep them up-to-date. Opportunity struck when events in Portugal led to the decolonisation of their colonies Angola and Mozambique; the medium-term outlook began to cloud for the white Rhodesian regime. So there were elections ('one man, one vote, once' said the whites) which were won by the former guerrillas. Our key observation is that Bishop Muzorewa, who had not gone into the resistance but had led an African party which dealt with the white regime, was the big loser at the polls. So the terrorist methodology while it did not in fact deal a crushing blow to the white regime stayed the course and succeeded in convincing black citizens that the former freedom fighters deserved to become the leaders of the new government. The 'convincing' is often a mix of genuine enthusiasm and strong-arm tactics.

Similarly and more recently parties with links to terrorism have done well in Northern Ireland (2005) and Palestine (2006). Who does not believe that the Western-imposed regimes in Afghanistan or Iraq will find it hard to win elections after the West has withdrawn …

Clandestine temptations

Terrorist groups are by necessity clandestine, and this situation has tempting overlaps with other clandestine activities: we have already mentioned the overlap with the secret services. The other main grey area is gangsterism. Criminals have useful skill-sets and maybe some are flattered to label themselves as revolutionaries! In practice many terrorist groups fund themselves by muscling in on rackets such as smuggling and prostitution or robbing banks and businesses. This can be an export business as well as in the home market! For instance a Balkan group needing hard currency could make a 'funding decision' to push drugs in German cities. A protection racket includes the elimination of any competing criminality, and this adds a useful message that 'we exercise police and tax functions around here'. The worst part of the criminal link is that the criminality often lasts longer than the cause — witness the Mafia which began as a 19th Century self-defence movement directed against feudal exploitation under the Spanish dynasty of Sicily.

International terrorism?

This is an even more slippery concept than terrorism itself. 'International' has almost become a bogey-word in phrases like 'international crime' 'international revolution' — even, in some mouths, 'international organisation'. Perhaps the problem is that things 'international' escape democratic accountability, law, policing and even tax … International terrorism does not fit into our definition in that the oppressor and victim are not so clear. Here are some ways to patch this up:

a) The 'cause' may be international rather than the method. For instance upholders of International Marxism could run terrorist campaigns in various countries: the individual country campaigns would fit our paradigm.

b) Cooperation in method is possible even if the causes are unrelated: the IRA has been accused of cooperating on equipment and training, criminal finance and even some cases of 'rent-a-terrorist'.

c) Cross-border terrorism over a disputed boundary is minimally international, though in our definition we saw it as quite likely derivative (state-sponsored) terrorism.

d) International also comes to mean 'hard to beat' when terrorist have created safe havens in one or more countries which the 'oppressor' of our definition cannot police: so hypothetically if the Tamil Tigers have fewer safe havens than the Kashmiris who want to escape Indian rule, the position of the former is more precarious.

Since 2001, international terrorism has been used as a label for Al-Quaeda. Funnily enough, Al-Quaeda in its beginnings does not our definition of a terrorist methodology because they are more a band of volunteers than champions who press gang for a repressed cause. They call people out of their regular lives to join a far more ambitious cause, the creation of a Muslim empire; their outrages are better thought of as declarations of war – indeed, the result of 9/11 was the international war to rid Afghanistan of the Taliban who had won a civil war and then formed a rogue state. After their defeat in 2002 the Taliban are now in a position to engage in standard-definition terrorism by infiltrating some specific Afghan constituency and putting them into a double bind.

At the time of writing, the Iraqi situation is hard to define as between civil war, resistance, and incipient terrorism, in particular with the aim of discrediting the political process sponsored by the occupying forces.

Romanticising terror

Terrorism's root cause is often assumed to be the repression and desperation of a group but many peoples who are in this state do not resort to terrorism. In particular rebellion might be a more natural response, and rebellion does not have to include terrorist methodology. Indeed in our definition, the terrorists are pressurizing the population they wish to 'save' and *planning* to usurp power for themselves after the coup – the assumption is that left to itself the oppressed population will prefer an easy life; a true popular uprising that will install a truly democratic system, or a military junta staging a putsch, do not fit our definition of terrorism (though they may lead to terrible bloodshed as the *Reign of Terror* did in late eighteenth century France).

Since terrorists often transfer the costs of their campaign onto the repressed constituency, they need to give themselves some redeeming qualities. Typically, terrorist movements seek in reply to show how noble their cause is, and how unacceptable its repression. So terrorist movements have an interest in talking up revolution, nationalism or whatever cause they champion. And state religion is often intertwined with nationalism. Also since terrorist groups need to be secret societies, some rite of initiation is common, in which the religious can play its part. So in a chapter on the morality of terrorism, we are forced to admit that terrorist movements often exhibit and defend a vibrant faith (including the dogmatic atheism of Marxism) . Of course, this does not make the faith bad or terrorism good.

A story from Jewish history gives us some clues on the role of religion and anger at the root of an uprising: The Maccabean Revolt was a typical double-pronged movement where the headline enemy was a Greek kingdom extending out of Syria while much of the business of the uprising consisted in intimidating compromising Jews; at the same time the Pharisaic religious movement was started. The revolt is supposed to have begun when the old priest Mattathias (father of Judas Maccabaeus) killed a Jew performing a pagan sacrifice as well as the Greek officer presiding, in a fit of righteous anger. We cannot know whether the beginning was premeditated or just happened, but the upshot was a guerrilla campaign which ended up establishing the family as the Hasmonean dynasty of Israel, the first time priesthood and kingship were combined in Judaea.

This story illustrates our theory that repression from one quarter plus righteous anger against compromisers are standard ingredients of the *résistance* motivation, while a crazy initial heroic outrage plus a zealous belief-system are acting as intensifiers. The Maccabees may not have been terrorists, but their story has analogies with the procedures and drivers that underlie terrorism. Though the Apocryphal Book of Maccabees naturally cheers for the insurgents, the New Testament reserves its judgement on that part of Jewish history: in fact the Hasmonean dynasty were a mixed blessing and the Pharisaic party that grew out of the uprising failed to welcome Jesus as Messiah.

Part of what the book of Maccabees is doing is legitimising the leader of the resistance and the cause of strict Judaism. Legitimacy is crucial for any cause being often gained *before* the terrorist method is adopted: remember Osama bin Laden's fight against the Russians; the IRA and the Ulster Volunteer Force (when they started in the early 20th century). Che Guevara before the Cuban revolution. And we find many modern examples of zealous belief (including humanist convictions) being emphasised as part of the 'cause'.

Again and again we see a romantic prospectus degenerating into a more cynical and brutal reality: a striking example was the Reign of Terror that followed the French Revolution. I would guess that outlook is worst when a revolution has some success at first before suffering its defeat; it is easier to keep a cause alive than to inaugurate a new one. If I may speculate about current affairs, whereas the Taliban first took power in Afghanistan through civil/political struggle, they may well try to make a comeback after the UN forces are withdrawn by adopting a terrorist methodology that succeeds in making the collaborators look weak, but comes far short of delivering the outcomes they promise.

The above observations yield a theoretical progression: cause - repression - terrorism -

crime (gangsterism or kleptocracy): the most likely moment for the terrorist choice to be made is after a cause has had a time of success in gaining followers, but the success has been noticed by the powers-that-be, then repressed or defeated; most of the followers accept to give up but the true believers have a personal call to fight on: the terrorist methodology actually does give a strong probability that the cause will live on — though survival can only grow into victory if the context changes (the repressing power weakens perhaps or a new ally appears).

The model of determined progression is a form of historicism quite close to the Communist / Hegelian idea that the fiercer the repression, the 'better' the revolution: it was easier to recruit for Communism in Tsarist Russia than in a liberal democracy. So an integral part of the terrorist methodology is that outrages produce crackdowns, and crackdowns bring in recruits, and the short-term aspirations of ordinary folk need to be sabotaged in favour of the long term and honourable cause. Such sacrificial thinking can be thought of as a competitor to religious passion (including both Christianity and other religions). On the other hand the religion of the repressive authority (say Eastern Orthodox Christianity) was branded as 'the opium of the people' because it overvalued accommodation with the old régime as against sacrifice for the cause. The marching song of Marxist revolution was *The Internationale* (key word!) which is clearly atheistic in stance.

The Roman-occupied Palestine of Jesus' day experienced plenty of *résistance* thinking which often has been a crucible of terrorist strategies. One of the twelve apostles was Simon the Zealot, a member of a party founded to carry on the tradition of the Maccabean Revolt. There are other New Testament allusions to terror-like activities: when Paul was saved from the mob by soldiers in Jerusalem [Acts 21:38], the Roman officer thought he was an Egyptian who had led a band of murderers (*sikarioi* – daggermen) out into the desert. Then a few weeks later a group of Jews took a vow to murder Paul no doubt because he was felt to be undermining the National Faith. Jesus always distanced himself from those advocating political intervention and warned Christians not to stay in Jerusalem for the coming revolts against the Romans. In the famous scene of Jesus' trial before Pilate, the crowd asks for Barabbas to be freed; now Barabbas had committed murder in an insurrection, so he could be considered a proto-terrorist and by implication that is not Jesus' way.

Many religious movements are historicist (= believe history is predetermined in a way favourable to the movement): in fact although the Islamic Jihadists have quite different values than the Marxists, their world views do have similarities: both camps see history as tending towards their victory which will be accompanied by a better government here on earth; they also are internationalists in that although nations may be part of the present reality of the world, they are less than the ideal state. While some Christians read their Bibles with historicist spectacles that predict a golden age for the church, most have typically responded to Marxist critique by rubbishing utopianism: God has decided not to impose perfection on the present world for, sadly, the sinfulness of mankind will always frustrate the birth pains of a better tomorrow. The Western mind is naturally suspicious of any revolution proposed by a self-selected group that foments trouble and imposes sacrifices on all. Ultimately, the end will not justify the means because "all who draw the sword will die by the sword" [Matt. 26:52]. Bottom line for Christians, the methodology of terrorism is just too dangerous in the hands of sinful humans, even those who can justly lay claim to have started out as heroes.

Counter-terrorism makes things worse

There is a general and a specialised meaning of the word counter-terrorism: the first just covers any actions that a government uses to control terrorists operating within its borders. The second, which is more interesting, is a like-for-like reply by a governing authority which is based on the notion that the best way to fight terrorism is to make the 'target constituency' of our definition more afraid of the government than of the terrorists. We are thinking of spectacular punishments and police brutality designed to intimidate ordinary folks.

Imagine a World War II French village which has just been the scene of a coup against the Occupying Forces. The method of counter-terrorism is to round up all the males from said village and massacre them publicly in cold blood: the overt rationale is that many of the executed know the perpetrators, and by hiding their identity, they in fact participate in the act. The real purpose is to scare the inhabitants in the surrounding land so that if they pick up *résistance* elements at work, they need to be aware that they run the terrible risk that if an attack occurs, the perpetrators may disappear into the maquis while they will be punished in their stead. So it is in their interest to report suspicions – anonymously of course, to avoid the equally dangerous label of collaborator.

So we deduce from this tougher concept of counter-terrorism a ready measure of who is winning in any war of terrorism versus counter-terrorism – it boils down to a simple-but-terrible question: *who is the target constituency more scared of?* Implacably executed, counter-terrorism probably wins more battles than the terrorists, but it can still lose the war, particularly if other states intervene or at least provide an impregnable place of refuge. Democracies in general find it hard to apply true counter-terrorism (except perhaps in far-flung colonies), which means that terrorism has a better chance of subverting a democracy than a dictatorship. In a voting situation, citizens will often vote for a partial capitulation if they think that there is a genuine chance of a quieter life.

The very unpleasantness of counter-terrorism amplifies the baneful consequences of terrorism itself. For lands where a terrorist/counter-terrorist struggle has been played out nearly always take a very long time to recover. Their economies have suffered from lack of investment (who would wish to invest in a troubled land?) and because the terrorist movement actively undermines the target constituency's enjoying the status quo. Unemployment and criminality become rife, authority is suspect and democratic checks and balances either nominal or non-existent. Consider the lands of the former Yugoslavia: they have gone through occupation by Austria, the Ottomans, the Nazis and finally a civil war in which the issue was decided by foreign intervention. In all these situations (except perhaps during the Royalist and Communist interludes), there has been an undercurrent of terrorist (or partisan) and repressive activity. After the centuries of pain, it remains to be seen whether the resulting set of new states will be viable economically and politically.

Generational warning

We saw in our study of Psalm 91 that it was a mistake to 'put God to the test' by volunteering for suicide attacks in the hope of a blessing: there is no doubt a blessing in sacrificing one's life for one's fellows, but only in reaction to someone's act of aggression. The difference is that there is an element of presumption or provocation in the devising of a suicide attack.

Generalising a little, we can, in Biblical terms, find a general condemnation of wilfully killing another person by treachery (Exodus 21:14). So any outrage is in danger of breaking of God's law, not by accident but wilfully, that is presumptuously. This concept of provocation, that is rebellion against God, will allow us to derive a hint as to why terrorism, even if it seems to work in terms of keeping a chosen cause alive, is unlikely to be blessed by God with a good outcome.

The hint comes a few psalms further on in Psalm 95:

> Today if you will hear his voice,
> harden not your heart
> as in the provocation (Heb Meribah)
> and in the day of temptation (Heb Massah)
> in the wilderness
> when your fathers tempted me,
> proved me and saw my work.
>
> Forty years long was I grieved with this generation, and said
> 'It is a people that do err in their heart,

for they have not known my ways;
unto whom I swore in my wrath,
that they should not enter into my rest.' [Ps
95:7b-11 KJV]

God decided that the nation of Israel that had
provoked him with faithlessness could not be
allowed into the Promised Land. My theory is
that, similarly, any group that decides to
provoke God by embarking on a campaign of
true terrorism condemns themselves and their
enemies to a generation, say 40 years, of unrest.

I'm going to take a risk and apply my theory
to situations still developing at the time of
writing: looking for instance at the situation in
Northern Ireland, the theory affirms that the
generation that started the current troubles in
the late 1960s is beginning to count for less; but
the most recent terrorist acts are only a few
years old, so that there are still probably 30
years before the place can safely be pro-
nounced normalised and peaceful. Zimbabwe
could have 15 years to go. Meanwhile in Palestine, the generation of Israelis that participated
in terrorism against the British during the
Mandate are in their dotage, while sadly the
Palestinian side is recruiting very young
people who may still be around for a full 40
years or more. Also, the present Israeli actions,
from 2002 onwards, can be classified as classic
counter-terrorism. On this basis the outlook for
peace and prosperity in the region is a long
way off. As long as there are trained fighters for

terrorism and counter-terrorism, both sides have a mechanism to halt any process of normalisation or to sabotage any peace conference where their arms are being twisted to offer compromises which they do not want. Also the dilapidated state of the Palestinian economy is virtually sure to provide fertile places to recruit terrorists for some time.

Today's terrorists may profit from hi-tech gadgetry plus civilisation's dependency on vulnerable networks such as electricity grids; but the time taken to heal the wounds is no shorter: it is still measured in human generations.

This study of Psalm 91 is more about defeating fear at a personal level, and getting the victory in advance on the battlefield of our minds. For if we can master our fear of terrorists, we are more likely to act wisely.

A well-known Old Testament passage illustrates the risks of being fearful: the story of the twelve spies in Numbers 13 and 14. As you remember, ten of the twelve scouts brought back a fearful report: "we are not able to go up against the people for they are stronger than we" [Num. 13:31]. They stirred up the people to murmur against Moses and God. The people of Israel then hear God's decree that they will die in the desert. The reaction is paradoxical and significant: they decide to make an attack on the enemy they feared so much without spiritual authority and without an achievable military plan. Arguably they also violated the custom of war of that age which was to demand surrender before attacking. The Bible specifically states that the decision was presumptuous [Numbers 14:44] .

The murmuring and the willingness to follow self-appointed leaders are typical of the terrorist motivation. The outrageous attack against the Amalekites was not terrorist in our defined sense, but it was suicidally foolish and the Israelites were duly defeated.

The lesson is that the correct handling of our fears is vital for if we lose the battle in our mind, and see our 'cause' losing out, the temptation will be strong to overcompensate by doing a desperate act, one that courts defeat unless God intervenes – that's an attempt to force God's hand. Or the conviction can grow out of fear that God does not love our particular constituency and has forgotten its problems. So self-appointed leaders decide to take action in God's place.

Our Psalm 91 then not only holds out the secret of overcoming our fears but also offers the seeds of an argument to challenge the false promises of the terrorist methodology. As we saw under Day 23 above, when Jesus refused to throw himself off the pinnacle of the temple, he was refusing the way of self-aggrandisement and a shortcut to power that avoided the cross of Calvary: the temptation to create salvation for oneself without identifying with the cross of

Christ encapsulates the 'error' that Christians see at the heart of terrorism. And perhaps not only Christians since Jews and Moslems alike recognise the Psalms as inspired.

What if Christians find themselves caught up in a cause that has turned to terrorist methodology? They are certainly not beyond redemption. In the Bible, the story of David's rise to kingship included a time as leader of a band of irregulars. While being hunted as a rebel, he twice could have killed King Saul by stealth but each time decided only to demonstrate his opponent's vulnerability. He certainly provoked fear in Saul and his general Abner [I Samuel 26] but 'valued life' [ibid, v.24].

Leaders need to command respect and sometimes, even for believers, earning respect will involve measured, proactive aggression. David showed how he could turn a weak position into a credible threat without resorting to outrage. Terrorism cannot be defended as being the only option.

WRAP UP

"Sleeping late?" said the voice on the phone. His voice was agitated, it was unusual for this guy to ring as he usually texts me.

" 'Morning, what's up?"

"Haven't you heard?" It was like I should but how could I have heard, since I was following the Rip Van Winkle solution to life problems.

"Many casualties, explosions right across London, in trains, on buses, shocking, close to where you live."

The phone cut off; there was silence. In the distance I could hear sirens, which were a common background noise in London but now they took on a new meaning. I picked up the phone and I rang out to find more information but I could not get a connection. I thought it must be the weight of calls, as the whole of London must be calling on their loved ones to see if they are OK. In the background, the noise of sirens came and went and a helicopter emitted its dull thud overhead while a soft drizzle speckled the closed window. Human communications break down at crisis moments: my next step, pray and get through to God Almighty in the secret place, and that's what I did.

Later on, the radio announcer said; 'A series of explosions have been reported in Edgware Road and King's Cross Area.' It was discovered that a knot of terrorists had come in via the King's Cross Station and as they unravelled they then fanned out north, south, west and east as if to create a flaming cross.

I mused on this and on King's Cross Station as the hub of entry. I thought of the Other King's cross, the cross of Jesus. I remembered 9/11 and the discovery by rescue workers at the base of the twin towers, the two iron girders, one from each building that when collapsing had formed a perfect cross.

I then recalled the conversion scene in *Pilgrim's Progress*:

> Now I saw in my dream, that the highway up which *Christian* was to go, was fenced on either side with a wall, and that wall was called *Salvation*. Up this way, therefore, did burdened *Christian* run, but not without great difficulty, because of the load on his back.

> He ran thus till he came at a place somewhat ascending, and upon that place stood a cross, and a little below, in the bottom, a sepulchre. So I saw in my dream, that just as *Christian* came up with the cross, his burden loosed from off his shoulders, and fell from off his back, and began to tumble, and so continued to do, till it came to the mouth of the sepulchre, where it fell in, and I saw it no more.

Then was *Christian* glad and lightsome, and said, with a merry heart, `He hath given me rest by his sorrow, and life by his death.' Then he stood still awhile to look and wonder; for it was very surprising to him, that the sight of the cross should thus ease him of his burden. He looked therefore, and looked again, even till the springs that were in his head sent the waters down his cheeks. Now, as he stood looking and weeping, behold three Shining Ones came to him and saluted him with *Peace be unto thee.* So the first said to him, *Thy sins be forgiven thee;* the second stripped him of his rags, and clothed him with change of raiment; the third also set a mark on his forehead, and gave him a roll with a seal upon it, which he bade him look on as he ran, and that he should give it in at the Celestial Gate. So they went their way.

Who's this? The Pilgrim. How! 'tis very true,
Old things are past away, all 's become new.
Strange! he's another man, upon my word,
They be fine feathers that make a fine bird.

Then Christian gave three leaps for joy, and went on singing—

Then I realised that Psalm 91 could be seen in the context of the cross of Jesus. God Almighty's personal promise to the believer of the ultimate shield of protection against the Biblical Prophecy of the ultimate terror, the Day of Judgement, the Day of Wrath. Was this the fiercest meaning of the 'fowler's snare'? Jesus did not say 'never fear': he said 'Do not be afraid of those who kill the body but cannot destroy the soul. Rather, be afraid of the One who can destroy both soul and body in Hell.' [Matthew 10:28 NIV]. But according to our psalm 'It will not come near you' and 'I will show you my salvation.'

Another day, another visit to the prayer chapel. On the streets the cold threat of terrorism and the imminent fear of violence still was everywhere. Even the people in the buses gave me cold stares and the cold shoulder as I tried to remain upright as the bus trundled along. I arrived just as the same priest I met at the start of the book was finishing off his sermon.

"The secret of success in life is not what you know but whom you know. There is a place where God can be met and worshipped. 'He who dwells in the secret place of the most high shall abide under the shadow of the Almighty.' For countless years many have come in times of joy and sorrow. Feel the presence of God there. 'Be still and know that I am God.' [Psalm 46:10]. That is the belief upon which a life can be built. It is within the context of the secret place that you can seek the person who can bring you through life victoriously. He has the power over the seen and unseen to deal with the realities of terror, violence and disease. In a world full of anxiety, frenzy, self-centredness and restlessness he is the place of security. In a world of weapons of mass destruction is God's weapon of mass protection. Welcome to the safest place in all the world!"

"Your teaching on Psalm 91 was fine!"

"Thank you, I hope you make it part of your prayers."

"Yes! What comes after Psalm 91?"

"92," the priest said dryly.

He continued, "It is believed that Psalm 92 is the thanksgiving of Psalm 91 ...The third jewel. Let's read it together."

Near the altar was the Lectern Bible, old and heavy. The pages were as large as the eagle's wings. We turn to Psalm 92:

"It is good to praise the LORD ..."

Notes

Abbreviations of Bible versions:

KJV . . . Authorized or King James Version

CEV . . . Contemporary English Version

NAS . . . New American Version

LB . . . Living BIBLE

NIV . . . New International Version

NKJV. . . New King James Version

GNB . . . Good News BIBLE

NRSV . . New Revised Standard Version

TM . . . The Message

TNEB . . The New English BIBLE

REB . . . Revised English BIBLE

AMP . . . Amplified BIBLE

You can find copyright notices for these
various translations on the web at bible.cc

BIBLIOGRAPHY

Sources of stories

The Promise Story: *Fragments from the Trenches* By Thomas Tiplady Chaplain to the Forces.

DAY 1   Idea taken from a feature on Sandy Kikwood in *Directions Magazine* (Elim) October 2005. Plus communication with him.

DAY 2   Jack McKee *Through Terror and Adversity* Alpha Publications 2002.

DAY 3   Source Author Quirk ; *James Stewart : Behind the scenes of a wonderful Life* 1997 Applause Publisher.

DAY 4   The Blondin story is well attested eg in the *Encyclopedia Britannica* of 1911, *Wikipedia* entry, websites.

DAY 5   Owd John Story from *The Times Archive*.

DAY 6   C H Spurgeon *Treasury of David*.

DAY 7   Yellowstone Story: found online [*'se non è vero, è ben trovato'!*].

DAY 8   Henri Nouwen Rembrandt's *The Prodigal*.

DAY 9   Association of Christian Military Fellowships website.

DAY 10 Philip Jacobson *The Times* 4/2/91.

DAY 11 From Mountain Movers Assemblies of God; used with permission from the Assemblies of God World Missions, 2002.

DAY 12 Lord Cravern Story taken from *The Treasury of David* by C H Sturgeon.

DAY 13 Story taken from *The Treasury of David* by C H Sturgeon.

DAY 14 W S Churchill (*Marlborough: His Life and Times* 1938, p163f).

Day 15 Marseille story from *The Percy Anecdotes* compiled in the early 1800s and available online.

DAY 16 *Martin Luther King* by Peter J Ling, Routledge 2002 p 51.

DAY 17 From Film *A Bridge too Far*.

DAY 18 Handley Page Floyd McClung *The Healing Power of God* Kingsway 1995.

DAY 19 *Shadow Of Wings* Source Joel News 10th May 1999

DAY 20 Daniel Defoe *Journal of the Plague in London*

DAY 21 *Life of Blessed Henry Suso* Ch.4. Thomas Aquinas from Dr Charles Singer, *The Legacy of Israel.*

DAY 22 David Gates' Story from Internet.

DAY 23   Dorothy Nicholls Story *Seeing Angels* by
Emma Heathcote, John Blake Publisher
2002, Page 55.

DAY 24 Taken from *Mary Slessor of Calabar*, by W
P Livingstone.

DAY 25 Moshe Dayan: source Michael B Oren in
The Atlantic Monthly June 12, 2002.

DAY 26 Heather Mercer & Diana Curry *Prisoners
Of Hope* Hodder and Stoughton 2002,
p132.

DAY 27 EAGLETS Story from Floyd McClung *The
Healing Power of God* Kingsway 1995.

DAY 28 Martin Luther reference

DAY 29 Joseph B Soloveitenik *The Lonely Man Of
Faith*

Corrie Ten Boom *The Hiding Place*,
Hodder & Stoughton

Commentaries used

The Oxford Bible Commentary
> Ed. Barton et al., Oxford University Press, 2000.

The New Jerome Biblical Commentary
> Editor Raymond E Brown et al. 1990 Geoffrey Chapman.

Peake's Commentary Of The Bible
> Black et al, 1962, Thomas Nelson.

Appendix: Adaptations

Imagine you are having a sandwich from a lunch box on a park bench when all of a sudden a skunk sits down beside you and starts to munch at your sandwiches. You have a series of choices: fight, which could turn out messy, flee or freeze – the last is the easiest and worst option!

One of the benefits of Psalm 91 is to be forearmed in emergencies and surprises: the language and choice of words allow you to adapt the psalm to your personal life/death situation, so that you can rehearse your response in the most appropriate way.

In the Secret Place you can seek the Lord Almighty and lift up the various threats and dangers visually. Psalm 91 gives you the framework. Why change the words? This is optional but Christ says that prayers need understanding. Also, God is intensely interested in the details of your life. Also dealings with violent incidents and confrontations creates mental stress and the bi-product can be intense destructive emotions which prey on you deep down. Imaginatively praying the situation to God could provide a better result than the alternative use of drugs etc. God may give insights or strategies etc.

Remember that from a visual point-of-view what you see and imagine are the same. So praying realistically is the aim of this section. What follows is a suggestion based on the *Good News* version:

1   Whoever goes to the Lord for safety, whoever remains under the protection of the Almighty,

2   Can say to him "You are my defender and protector. You are my God, in you I trust."

> [In the next verse instead of repeating "all hidden dangers" insert the dangers you are concerned about at present: e.g. bullying, abuse, terrorist threats, disease or diagnostic testing, panic attacks, political or even theological skulduggery]

3   He will keep you safe from all hidden dangers and from all deadly diseases.

4   He will cover you with his wings; you will be safe in his care; his faithfulness will protect and defend you.

5   You need not fear any dangers at night, or sudden attacks during the day.

6   Or the plagues that strike in the dark or the evils that kill in daylight.

> [Reflect with God on the seen/predictable and unseen/surprise aspects of your situation. Include the flashes of unreason and anger in yourself as well as in others: has someone spread rumours; were you publicly snubbed?]

7   A thousand may fall dead beside you, ten
    thousand all around you, but you will not be
    harmed.

8   You will look and see how the wicked are
    punished.

      [A moment for honesty: reflect on the moral
      side of things and confess any areas where you
            feel in need of forgiveness yourself. Give
         thanks for any privileged position and take
         time to pray for those who persecute you]

9   You had made the Lord your defender, the
    Most High your protector.

10 And so no disaster will strike you, no violence
    will come near your home.

      [It is natural to pray protection for your family
            and loved ones as well as for yourself]

11 God will put his angels in charge of you to
    protect you wherever you go.

12 They will hold you up with their hands, to
    keep you from hurting your feet on the stones.

13 You will trample down lions and snakes; fierce
    lions and poisonous snakes.

      [Attack is sometimes the best form of defence.
            Don't be shy about lifting up to God any
      actions you are undertaking in the light of your
      faith in God's promises; also tell God about the
            spiritual attacks and temptations you face]

14 God says, "I will save those who love me and will protect those who acknowledge me as Lord.

15 When they call to me, I will answer them; when they are in trouble I will be with them. I will rescue them and honour them.

16 I will reward them with long life; I will save them.

[A hint of Eternity puts our present troubles in perspective. After all this, as suggested above, Psalm 92 strikes a suitable chord of thanks]

Appendix: Website

On the website www.terror-rest.net I will be putting up various links to other sites of interest and versions of scripture and musical renditions. I am also working on non-book product such as cards or clothing lines associated with Psalm 91.

I would be glad to receive ideas for other links at info@terror-rest.net.